P9-CEE-191

fabulous PAINTED FURNITURE

fabulous PAINTED FURNITURE

Mickey Baskett

Sterling Publishing Co., Inc.
New York

Prolific Impressions Production Staff:

Editor: Mickey Baskett
Creative Design: Susan E. Mickey
Copy: Phyllis Mueller
Graphics: Dianne Miller, Karen Turpin
Styling: Kirsten Werner Jones, Lenos Key
Photography: Jerry Mucklow, Pat Molnar
Administration: Jim Baskett

Every effort has been made to insure that the information presented is accurate. Since we have no control over physical conditions, individual skills, or chosen tools and products, the publisher disclaims any liability for injuries, losses, untoward results, or any other damages which may result from the use of the information in this book. Thoroughly read the instructions for all products used to complete the projects in this book, paying particular attention to all cautions and warnings shown for that product to ensure their proper and safe use.

Library of Congress Cataloging-in-Publication Data Available

10 9 8 7 6 5 4 3 2 1

Published by Sterling Publishing Company, Inc.
387 Park Avenue South, New York, N.Y. 10016

Produced by Prolific Impressions, Inc.
160 South Candler St., Decatur, GA 30030

Distributed in Canada by Sterling Publishing
c/o Canadian Manda Group, One Atlantic Avenue, Suite 105
Toronto, Ontario, Canada M6K 3E7
Distributed in Great Britain and Europe by Cassell PLC
Wellington House, 125 Strand, London WC2R 0BB, England
Distributed in Australia by Capricorn Link (Australia) Pty. Ltd.
P.O. Box 704, Windsor, NSW 2756 Australia

Printed in the USA

ISBN 0-8069-2251-6

Acknowledgements

Mickey Baskett thanks the following for their generous contributions:

Plaid Enterprises, Inc.
3223 Westech Dr.
Norcross, GA 30092
www.plaidonline.com
For supplying artists with painting products such as FolkArt® Acrylic Colors; Durable Colors™ indoor/outdoor paint; FolkArt® varnishes; Apple Barrel® indoor/outdoor acrylic bottle paints; Decorator Products® tools and stamps.

JM Original Creations
Norcross, GA 30071
770-248-9010
For unfinished wooden furniture.

CONTENTS

Introduction

With paint, stain, and paper, you can give new life to old furniture or transform inexpensive, unfinished pieces into fantastic and fanciful works of art that add a personal touch to the rooms of your home.

The projects in this book present an array of techniques for decorating and refurbishing chairs, tables, chests of drawers, cabinets, and kids' furniture. They showcase a range of styles and designs – rustic and elegant, simple and sophisticated, restrained and ornate – that employ decorative painting, decoupage, crackling, distressing, gold leafing, sponging, staining, stamping, and stenciling.

Paint a chair as a focal point for a room. Use stain to create faux parquet on a wooden chest. Give new life to a tired table with colorful painted designs. Stencil with gold leafing on an armoire. Stamp a leaf in autumn colors on a crackled, rustic blanket chest. Decorate fun furniture for kids that they'll want to pass on to their own children. Use the ideas presented with each project as a springboard for designing and personalizing.

There are step-by-step instructions and numerous photographs to guide you. Have fun being your own furniture designer!

Mickey Baskett

Supplies for Furniture Preparation

For Cleaning & Stripping

Mild Detergent or Bubble Bath:

If you are going to paint your piece of furniture, you will find that stripping it is not necessary – you just need to clean it up. To remove dirt, dust, cobwebs, etc., use a cleaner that does not leave a gritty residue. Effective cleaners include **mild dishwashing detergent** and **bubble bath**. Mix the cleaner with water and wash the furniture with a cellulose sponge. Rinse and wipe dry with soft cloth rags.

Paint Thinner:

Use **paint thinner** and a **steel wool pad** to remove waxy buildup on stained wooden pieces and old varnish or shellac.

Paint Stripper:

There are several reasons you may wish to strip a piece of furniture. If you plan to stain, pickle, or color wash the piece, you will need to get down to bare wood. And if the piece of furniture is covered with layers of badly flaking, wrinkled, or uneven paint that can't be sanded smooth, stripping is necessary. There are many brands of paint strippers available at do-it-yourself and hardware stores. Apply **paint stripper** with a brush. When the paint begins to wrinkle and lift, remove it with a **paint scraper**.

For Sanding & Filling

Sandpaper:

Sandpaper is available in different grits for different types of sanding. Generally, start with medium grit sandpaper, and then use fine grit to sand before painting. Between coats of paint, sand lightly with fine or extra fine sandpaper.

Sanding Block:

This wooden block that sandpaper is wrapped around aids smooth sanding on flat surfaces.

Electric Sander:

A handheld **electric finishing sander** aids in sanding large, flat areas. Use wet/dry sandpaper and wet it to keep down dust. Wipe away sanding dust with a **tack cloth.**

Wood Filler:

Wood filler or wood putty, applied with a **putty knife**, is used to fill cracks, holes, dents, and nicks for a smooth, even painting surface. You can use wood filler on raw wood furniture or previously painted or stained furniture. Let dry and sand smooth.

For Priming & Base Painting

Primer:

A **primer** fills and seals wood and helps paint to bond properly. A **stain blocking primer** keeps an old finish from bleeding through new paint. This is especially necessary if you have a dark piece of furniture and want to paint it a light color. Always allow primer to dry thoroughly before base painting.

You can make your own primer by slightly thinning white flat latex wall paint with water. One coat on an old painted or stained piece helps give the surface some "tooth" so the base paint will adhere properly.

Paint for Base Painting:

Base paint is the first layer of paint applied to a surface after a primer. Base paint your furniture piece with **latex wall paint in an eggshell or satin finish**, **acrylic indoor/outdoor paint**, or **acrylic craft paint.** Brush on the paint, using long, smooth strokes. Work carefully to avoid runs, drips, or sags.

All the painting in this book was done with waterbase paints. Today's formulas provide as much wear-and-tear protection as oil-based paints.

Brushes:

Base paint can be applied with a **foam brush** or **bristle paint brush.** For painting details or smaller areas, use a 1" **craft brush.** For painting larger flat areas, a **foam roller** is a good choice.

Miscellaneous Supplies:

Wear **latex gloves** to protect your hands from cleaners, solvents, and paints. These tight-fitting gloves, available at hardware stores, paint stores, and home improvement centers, will not impair your dexterity.

Masking Tape:

This often under-valued supply is essential for furniture decorating. Use **masking tape** to mask off areas for painting, to make crisp lines, and to protect previously painted areas.

Pictured clockwise, beginning at bottom left: 1" craft brush, 2" foam brush, 1-1/2" bristle brush, foam roller, acrylic indoor/outdoor paint, paint thinner, steel wool, latex gloves, paint scraper, paint remover, stain blocking primer, masking tape in a tape dispenser, handheld electric sander, sandpaper, sanding block, putty knife, wood filler, cellulose sponge, soft cloth rag, liquid detergent.

WAGNER
Mask-It™
Thinner
DANGER!
32 FL OZ (ONE QT) .95 LITER

Preparation

New Unfinished Wood Furniture

New unfinished wood furniture requires less preparation than old furniture – often sanding and priming are all that's necessary.

Step 1 – Sanding:

Sand the furniture with fine grit sandpaper, sanding with the grain of the wood, to remove rough edges and smooth the surface. Use a sanding block (**photo 1**) or handheld electric sander on flat surfaces. Hold the paper in your hand on curved areas. Remove dust with a tack cloth or a dry dust cloth. Don't use a damp cloth – the dampness could raise the grain of the wood.

On some furniture, glue may have seeped out of the joints. It's important to remove any glue residue – paint won't adhere to it. If possible, sand away the dried glue. If sanding doesn't remove it, scrape it lightly with a craft knife.

Step 2 – Sealing (Optional):

If there are knots or dark places on the piece, seal them with clear sealer or shellac (**photo 2**). Let dry completely. This will keep sap or residue from bleeding through the base paint.

Photo 1 *– Sanding with a sanding block.*

Photo 2 *– Sealing with shellac.*

Step 3 – Filling (Optional):

If your piece has nail holes, gaps, or cracks, fill them with wood filler or wood putty, using a putty knife. Smooth the material as much as possible and remove any excess before it dries. Follow manufacturer's recommendations regarding drying time. When dry, sand smooth. Wipe away dust.

Step 4 – Priming:

Paint the piece with a coat of diluted flat white latex wall paint (mixed by adding about 10% water to paint) or spray primer (**photo 3**). Let dry thoroughly. Sand with fine sandpaper. Wipe away dust with a tack cloth.

Step 5 – Base Painting:

The base paint is the foundation upon which you build your decorative effects – you can sponge over it, rag it, add decorative painted elements, distress it, or antique it. Because it is your foundation, you want it to be smooth and to have thoroughly covered the wood. Apply base paint with a small roller or a wide fine-bristled brush. Apply one light coat and allow it to dry. Sand with fine sandpaper to smooth the surface. Apply a second coat and allow it to dry thoroughly. You are now ready to enjoy your piece or to add additional decorative effects.

***Photo 3** – Applying a primer.*

Why Choose Waterbase Paints?

Because waterbase paints have so many advantages and are so readily available, they were used for all the projects in this book. Some advantages include:

- They have less odor because they contain far less solvent than oil-base paints, and so are much less apt to provoke headache or nausea. Some types are considered non-toxic.
- Cleanup is easy with soap and water, so the painter is not exposed to solvents in the cleaning of tools or brushes.
- They are safer to use indoors and not nearly as polluting as solvent-based paints in their manufacturing process or in the volatile organic compounds (VOCs) they release after application.

Old Furniture to be Painted

Chances are there's a piece of furniture that's languished for years in your attic, basement, or garage that's a perfect candidate for painting. Tag and yard sales and used furniture stores are other good sources of old furniture. When selecting an old furniture piece, choose one in sound condition. If the legs are wobbly or the drawers stick, make repairs before painting. Repair loose joints with wood glue. If extensive repairs are needed, seek the services of a professional.

When an old piece of furniture is to receive a painted finish, very often all the piece needs is cleaning and sanding. A primer coat may be necessary if the piece has a glossy finish. If the finish is in very bad condition or the varnish is wrinkled and chipped, you may choose to strip it. Stripping is usually a last resort.

A good rule of thumb is to work with what you have. If your old piece of furniture has a dark finish, perhaps you'll decide to paint it dark green to minimize the amount of preparation you'll need to do, instead of trying to cover up the dark finish with a light paint color. Study your piece to determine how much preparation needs to be done.

Precautions & Tips

- Read product labels carefully and observe all manufacturer's recommendations and cautions.
- **Always** work in a well-ventilated area or outdoors.
- Wear gloves to protect your hands.
- Wear a dust mask or respirator to protect yourself from dust and fumes.
- Use a piece of old or scrap vinyl flooring for a work surface. Vinyl flooring is more protective and more convenient than layers of newspaper or plastic sheeting. Paint or finishes can seep through newspapers, and newspapers always get stuck to your shoes. Plastic sheeting is slippery. Spills can be wiped up quickly from vinyl, and nothing will seep through it to your floor. Small pieces of vinyl can be purchased inexpensively as remnants at floor covering stores and building supply centers.
- Dispose of solvents properly. If in doubt of how to dispose of them, contact your local government for instructions. Do not pour solvents or paint strippers down drains or toilets.

Step 1 – Removing Hardware:

Before cleaning or sanding, remove all hardware, such as door and drawer pulls. (**photo 1**) Depending upon your piece and what you're planning to do, it also may be necessary to remove hinges, doors, drawers, or mirrors. This is also the time to remove upholstered seats from chairs. Drawer pulls and knobs should be painted or treated while they are detached.

Photo 1 *– Removing hardware.*

Step 2 – Cleaning:

The next step is removing accumulated dust, grease, and grime. Sometimes careful cleaning is all that's needed before painting. To clean, mix a little mild detergent or bubble bath with water in a bucket or basin. Using a household sponge, wash the piece with the soapy solution (**photo 2**). Rinse with clear water. Wipe the piece with soft cloth rags to remove surface water. Allow to air dry until the piece is completely dry.

If your piece has years of wax buildup or is covered with shellac or varnish that has cracked or worn unevenly, use a solvent to provide a thorough cleaning. This is necessary because wax repels waterbased paints and shellac and varnish are poor undercoats for paint. Pour a solvent such as paint thinner, mineral spirits, or a liquid sandpaper product in a metal can or enamel bowl. Wear protective gloves. Dip a steel wool pad in the solvent and rub the surface (**photo 3**). Rinse the pad in solvent occasionally as you work, and replace the solvent in your container when it gets dirty. When you're finished, allow the piece to air dry.

Step 3 – Sanding:

An important step in the preparation process, sanding dulls the old finish so new paint will adhere properly and creates a smooth surface for painting. To sand the piece smooth, start with medium grit sandpaper, then use fine grit. Always sand in the direction of the grain. Wrap the sandpaper around a sanding block on flat surfaces (**photo 4**). Use a handheld electric finishing sander on larger flat areas, such as tops and shelves (**photo 5**). Hold the paper in your hand when working in tight areas or on curves (**photo 6**). Wipe away dust with a tack cloth. To remove sanding dust from crevices and tight areas, use a brush or a vacuum cleaner.

Photo 2 – Washing a piece with a mild soapy solution.

Photo 4 – Sanding a flat surface with sandpaper wrapped around a sanding block.

Photo 3 – Removing wax buildup with a steel wool pad dipped in paint thinner.

Photo 5 – Sanding a flat surface with a hand-held electric finishing sander.

Sanding Tips

- When sanding old paint that may contain lead, use wet/dry sandpaper and wet the paper while sanding to prevent creating dust.
- **Always** wear a mask when sanding to prevent inhaling dust.

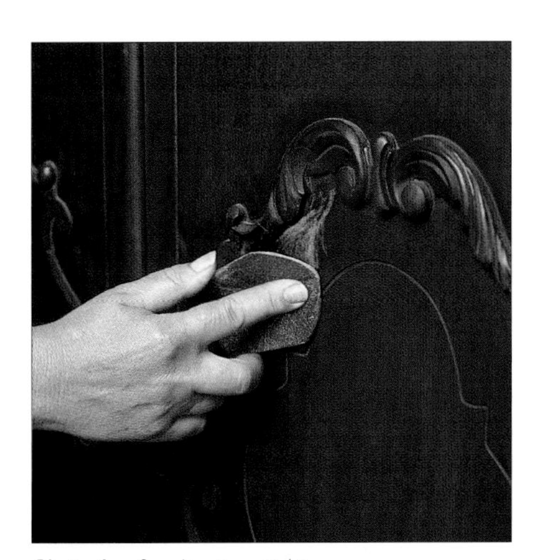

Photo 6 – Sanding in a tight area.

Continued on page 14

Continued from page 13, Old Furniture to be Painted

Step 4 – Filling and Smoothing:

Fill cracks, dents, nicks, and holes with a paste wood filler or wood putty. Apply the paste with a putty knife, smoothing the material as much as possible and removing any excess before it dries. Follow manufacturer's recommendations regarding drying time. If necessary, apply a second time and let dry thoroughly. Sand smooth when dry. Wipe away dust.

Photo 7 – *Filling a crack with wood putty.*

Step 5 – Priming or Undercoating:

Priming or undercoating seals the wood and prevents dark areas from showing through a light colored base paint. Don't use a primer if you intend to apply a stain or color wash. And if you're planning to create a distressed finish that involves sanding through the layers of paint or that will reveal some of the bare wood, don't use a primer.

For most finishes, flat white latex wall paint that has been diluted with a little water is an appropriate primer. Mix the paint with a little water (about 10%) to make it go on smoothly.

If your piece has a dark stained or varnished surface, apply a stain blocking white primer so the dark stain or varnish won't bleed through your new paint. Stain blocking primers are also available as sprays.

To make your own stain blocking primer, mix equal amounts of white latex wall paint and acrylic varnish. Sponge this mixture over the surface of your piece.

Allow primer to dry overnight. Sand again, lightly, for a smooth surface. Wipe away dust. You're ready to paint!

Photo 8 – *Applying white primer with a bristle paint brush.*

Step 6 – Base Painting:

The base paint is the foundation upon which you build your decorative effects – you can sponge over it, rag it, add decorative painted elements, distress it, or antique it. There are a number of paints that will work for basepainting. I prefer an eggshell finish or satin finish acrylic or latex paint. Craft shops or hardware stores sell acrylic or latex paints in small portions that work great for painting furniture. Even wall paint will be fine – as long as it has a satin finish rather than a flat finish. Indoor/outdoor paint with a matte or satin finish is also a wonderful basepaint.

Because it is your foundation, you want it to be smooth and to have thoroughly covered the old paint or finish. Apply base paint with a small roller or a wide fine-bristled brush. Apply one light coat and allow it to dry. Sand with fine sandpaper to smooth the surface. Apply a second coat and allow it to dry thoroughly. If any of the old finish still shows, apply a third coat. Allow to dry. You are now ready to enjoy your piece or to add additional decorative effects.

Photo 9 – *Base painting after primer.*

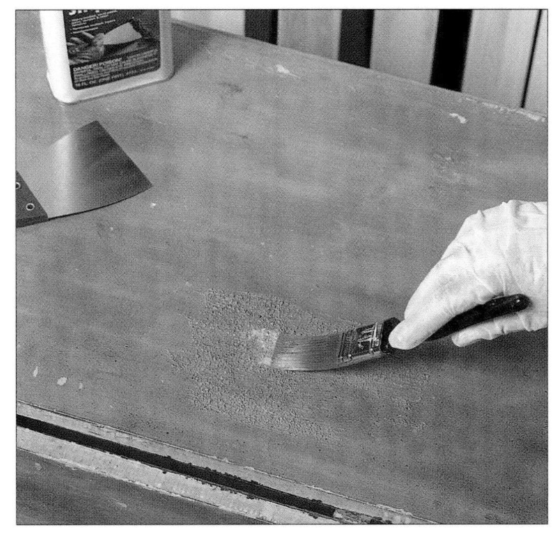

Photo 1 – Applying the stripper with a bristle brush.

Optional Stripping

Furniture that was previously painted doesn't need stripping if the finish is sound and not too thick. However, if the existing paint or varnish is chipped, blistered, or cracked, or if the original finish was poorly applied, or if the paint on the piece is so thick it's obscuring the lines or details of the piece, stripping is warranted. You can, of course, have the stripping done by a professional – all you'll need to do is sand the piece afterward. Sometimes it costs less to have a professional do the job than it would to buy the supplies and equipment to do the job yourself.

If you wish to strip the piece yourself, purchase a liquid, gel, or paste product specifically made for the job you're doing. (These generally are labeled "stripper" or "paint remover" and may be waterbased or solvent-based.) Read the label carefully and follow the instructions exactly. Work in a well-ventilated space and wear gloves, goggles, and protective clothing.

Step 1 – Applying the Stripper:

Apply an even layer of stripper to the surface with a bristle brush (**photo 1**) in the direction of the grain of the wood. Wait the recommended amount of time. The old paint or finish will soften, look wrinkled, and start to lift. Be patient! Chemical strippers give the best results when you allow them enough time to work properly.

Photo 2 – Lifting the softened old finish with a paint scraper.

Step 2 – Removing the Old Finish:

Use a paint scraper to lift the old finish from the surface (**photo 2**), again working in the direction of the grain. Be careful not to gouge or scrape the surface as you work. On curves, in crevices, and on carved areas, remove the old finish with steel wool, an old bristle brush, toothpicks, or rags.

Finishing Your Project

If you haven't used indoor/outdoor paint for your decorating, you will want to give your finished piece a protective coating. Use waterbase varnishes and sealers that are compatible with acrylic paints for sealing and finishing. They are available in brush on and spray formulations. Choose products that are non-yellowing and quick drying.

Varnishes and sealers are available in a variety of finishes – matte, satin, and gloss. Satin is my favorite. It gives a nice luster but doesn't emphasize uneven brush strokes like a gloss finish can.

Apply the finish according to the manufacturer's instructions. Several thin coats are better than one thick coat (**photo 3**). Let dry between coats according to the manufacturer's recommendations. A furniture piece such a breakfast table, which will receive a lot of use, will need more coats of sealer or varnish for protection than a piece that is decorative or receives less use.

Photo 3 – Applying waterbase varnish with a foam brush.

Decorating Techniques

There are many techniques you can use to decorate your furniture. This book will show you many options, such as:

- Decorative Painting
- Decoupage
- Crackling
- Distressing
- Gold Leafing
- Sponging
- Staining
- Stamping
- Stenciling

The techniques are easy to accomplish and inexpensive to complete. The pages on each technique include information on the basic supplies you'll need and step-by-step instructions with numerous how-to photographs.

You can refer to this section for basic information when you start a project, as each project includes a list of the techniques used in creating it.

Decorative Painting

Painted designs are a wonderful way to create a decorative focal point for a room or a coordinated, custom look on furniture. Just looking through the pages of this book shows you how versatile painted designs can be.

Basic Supplies

Acrylic Craft Paints

Acrylic craft paints, sold in 2 oz. bottles, are used to paint the designs. There are a variety of brands of these acrylic craft paints that are formulated especially for decorative painting or design painting. They are thicker and more opaque with pigment than most acrylic paints. They come in a wide array of pre-mixed colors and are available at craft shops or departments. They are inexpensive to buy and easy to use, even for beginners. Cleanup is easy with soap and water.

Artist Brushes

You'll need an assortment of artist's paint brushes – rounds, liners, and flats in various sizes – for decorative painting. Use round or flat brushes for applying color, flat brushes for blending, shading and highlighting, and liner brushes for painting details and outlining. You will find these in art stores or in art or decorative painting departments of craft shops.

Palette

For loading your brushes, you'll need a palette or a disposable foam plate. A "Sta-Wet" palette is best to use when painting with acrylic paints. This type of palette has a wet sponge under a piece of wax coated paper. This keeps the paints moist and ready to use.

Water container

A water container is needed for rinsing brushes.

Pattern Transferring Supplies

Patterns are included for all the designs. You can paint your design free-hand by using the pattern as a guide, or you can transfer the pattern directly to your furniture piece. Use **tracing paper** and a **pencil** to trace the design from the book. Then you can enlarge or reduce the pattern as needed to fit your surface. Use **transfer paper** and a **stylus** to transfer the design to the surface.

Waterbase. Heavy pigmentation, smooth texture. For use on all paintable surfaces. Shake well. Colors may be intermixed. Let dry 1 hour between coats. Clean up with soap and water. Made in USA.
À base d'eau. Forte pigmentation, grain lisse. S'utilise sur toutes les surfaces acceptant la peinture. Bien agiter. Les couleurs sont mélangeables. Laisser sécher pendant 1 heure entre les couches. Nettoyage à l'eau et au savon. Fabriqué aux USA.
Con base de agua. Pigmentación pesada, textura lisa. Para uso en todas las superficies pintables. Agite bien. Los colores se pueden mezclar. Deje que se seque una hora antes de aplicar la segunda mano. Limpie con agua y jabón. Hecho en EE.UU.

Steps to Successful Decorative Painting

1. Prepare the Furniture.

Prepare the furniture piece according to the instructions in the "Preparation" section.

2. Trace & Transfer Pattern.

Trace pattern from book on tracing paper (**photo 1**). Enlarge or reduce pattern to fit, if needed. Transfer design to surface, using transfer paper and a stylus (**photo 2**).

3. Prepare Palette.

Squeeze puddles of paint on a palette or foam plate. Leave space on the palette for loading brushes and blending colors. A "Sta-Wet" palette will keep your paints moist and ready for painting.

Photo 1. Tracing the pattern.

Photo 2. Transferring design to surface.

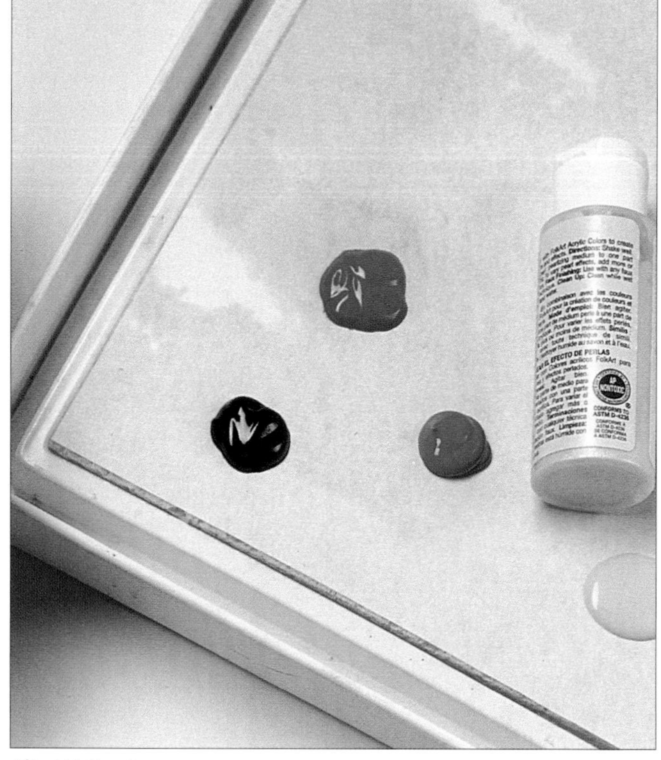

"Sta-Wet" palette

Photo 3. Lifting the transfer paper reveals the transferred design, ready for painting.

Photo 4 – Basecoat the design area.

Photo 5 – Float the shading on design.

Photo 6 – Float the highlights on design.

4. Paint the Design

You can paint the designs shown using a very simple technique I call "colorbook painting," which is merely painting the areas of the design one color. Then using black paint or a permanent marker to outline the design. Or, you can use a decorative painting technique where areas of the design are shaded and highlighted.

• Basecoat the design area.
The basecoat is the first layer of paint that a part of a design receives. For example, if you are painting a flower and leaf design, you would first fill in the entire leaf with a green color as specified. A good rule of thumb is to use the largest brush you can handle that fits the area of the design you're painting.

• Float the shading on design.
Shading creates shadows, darkens and deepens color, and makes an area recede. In decorative painting, one side of painted subject is often shaded to add depth and dimension. To "float" the shading, load the brush with a floating medium, or a little water. Load brush with the green color that is the predominant color of design (for example: the green basecoat color of the leaf). Then pull one side of the brush through a darker shade of color to load just the side of the brush. Blend the brush back and forth on the palette to blend the colors. Apply this to the design, with the dark side of the brush on the outside, or dark side, of the design.

• Float the highlighting on the design.
Highlighting creates dimension by adding light in the form of a lighter color and makes an area seem closer. This technique is done in the same way as "floating shading." You will load the brush with the predominant color, then sideload the brush with a lighter shade of color.

• Add details.
Details are painted last. The amount of detail depends on the particular design. Most often, this refers to using a thin liner brush loaded with black paint to add definition to the design.

Optional – Outlining: Outlining is adding a dark line around the edge of a design for emphasis. Outlining, usually done with a liner brush, adds emphasis to designs. Outlining also may be done with a fine tip permanent marker.

Decoupage

Decoupage – the art of applying paper or fabric to surfaces and covering the surface with a finish – can be used to add texture, color, and designs to surfaces. You can use the decoupage technique to completely cover a surface or add spot motifs with cutouts.

Basic Supplies

Decoupage Finish

Traditionally, decoupage was done with glue and layers of varnish. Today's decoupage medium is a clear-drying liquid that is used as both glue and finish. You can find decoupage finish in most craft shops or craft departments.

Designs to Decoupage

Gift wrap, art prints, calendars, photocopies of your photographs, and pages from books of clip art (find them at art supply stores) can all be used. You also can find papers especially for decoupaging at crafts stores. Fabric and fabric cutouts can also be used for decoupage. Since most of today's decoupage finishes are water-based, you should not have any problem with the printing ink bleeding. If you are not sure, then use a spray sealer to lightly spray on the printed design before cutting out.

Cutting Tools

A pair of good quality, small, sharp scissors are essential for success in cutting out designs. A craft knife with a sharp #11 blade and a self-healing mat are useful for cutting interior areas of motifs and large pieces of paper.

Brushes

Use a foam brush, or a very fine-bristled varnish brush to apply decoupage medium.

Pictured clockwise from top left: _Acrylic craft paint for basecoating project; decoupage finish; Giftwrap and greeting cards for design images to decoupage; decoupage finish; scissors; palette and foam brush._

Here's How to Decoupage

1. Cut out motifs from paper or fabric with small scissors.

2. Either apply decoupage medium to the back of cutout motifs with an applicator brush and position on the surface **or** *brush decoupage medium on the surface and position paper pieces. Let dry.*

3. Apply at least two coats of decoupage medium over the paper or fabric to finish. Let dry between coats.

Fish images cut from wrapping paper and decoupaged to chair seat.

Crackling

The age and character that naturally comes from years of wind and weather can be easily created on painted surfaces with crackle medium.

There are two ways to create crackled finishes:

One-color crackle uses latex paint as a basecoat. Crackle medium is applied and allowed to dry. A clear waterbase varnish is used as a topcoat. The crackle medium causes the varnish to form cracks. When dry, the cracks are rubbed with an antiquing medium, which imparts color to the cracks.

Two-color crackle uses two latex paint colors – one for the basecoat and one for the topcoat. The crackle medium is applied between the coats of paint, causing the topcoat to crack and reveal the basecoat.

Basic Supplies

Paint

Use latex paint (for larger projects) or acrylic craft paint (for smaller projects or areas). You'll need one paint color for the basecoat in the one-color method and two colors (one basecoat, one topcoat) for the two-color method.

Crackle Medium

Crackle medium is a clear liquid. It does not crack, but any waterbased medium (paint or varnish, or example) applied on top of it reacts by shrinking and forming cracks, creating the distinctive crackled look.

Tools

Use foam brushes to apply paint and crackle medium. Use a sponge to rub antiquing medium or tinted glaze into the cracks for the one-color method.

Varnish

For the one-color method, apply a brush-on clear water-base varnish over the crackle medium.

Antiquing

For one-color method, rub an antiquing medium or tinted glaze (neutral glazing medium + color) into the cracks in the varnish.

Here's How – One-Color Crackle

1. Apply the basecoat. Let dry.

2. Apply the crackle medium. Let dry. Apply clear varnish atop the crackle medium. Cracks will form as varnish dries. Let the varnish dry completely.

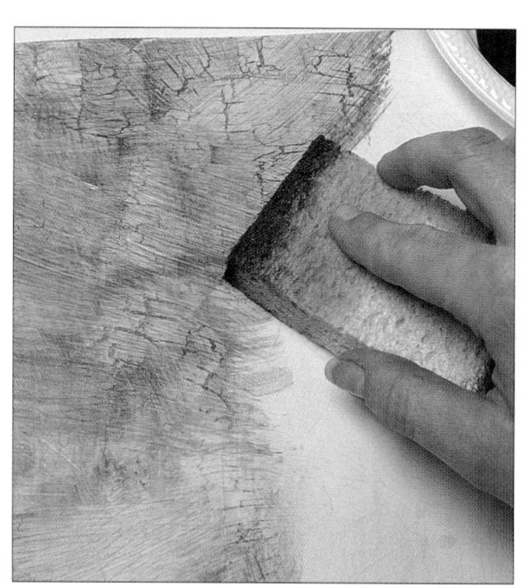

3. Rub antiquing medium over the surface to darken the cracks.

Here's How – Two-Color Crackle

1. Apply the first paint color. Let dry.

2. Apply crackle medium. Let dry.

3. Apply second paint color. Cracks will form as the paint dries.

Two-color crackle technique with white basecoat and blue top coat.

Distressing

Distressed finishes add the character imparted by use and age. You can create a simple distressed finish by painting a piece with layers of color and sanding or scraping the piece after the paint has dried. This removes some of the paint, exposing layers of color and allowing some of the wood to show. **Don't** use a primer if you're planning to distress a piece and sand down to the wood.

Basic Supplies

Paint

You'll need two (or more) colors of latex or acrylic paint to create the layers of color.

Sandpaper

Use sandpaper to remove paint and reveal the layers. You'll need medium, medium-fine, and fine grit sandpapers.

Wax stick

Applying wax to the surface between coats of paint makes the succeeding coats easier to remove. You can buy a wax stick for this purpose from a crafts store or use a piece of a candle or a paraffin block.

Metal scraper

A metal scraper or putty knife can be used to remove paint from the surface and to create dings and dents characteristic of wear and age.

Brushes

Use foam brushes or flat bristle brushes for applying the layers of paint.

Tack cloth

Use a tack cloth to wipe away sanding dust.

Sanding Tips

- Sand more on the edges of the piece – concentrating your efforts in places where wear would normally occur over time – and less on flat areas for a more natural appearance.
- Don't use a sanding block or an electric sander – you want an uneven look. Holding the sandpaper in your hand is best and allows you more control.
- Use medium or medium-fine grit sandpaper to remove more paint, fine grit sandpaper to remove less.
- It's best to begin slowly and err on the side of removing too little paint rather than too much. You can always sand again to remove more. Stop when the result pleases you.

Here's How

1. Paint piece with first paint color. Let dry.

2. Apply wax to areas of piece where wear would normally occur.

3. Paint with second paint color. Let dry.

4. Sand and/or scrape paint to reveal paint layers and/or bare wood. After sanding, use a tack cloth to wipe away dust. ❑

Gold Leafing

Gold leafing is an elegant, traditional way to add a warm metallic glow to surfaces. Once you try it and see how easy it is to add luxurious beauty to a piece, you will be hooked. Metal leafing sheets and leaf adhesive are easy to use and available at art supply and crafts stores.

Basic Supplies

Paint

Use dark red acrylic paint as a base paint for gold leafing if you are planning to apply leaf to an entire surface. The red paint adds a rich base and gives depth to the metal leafing.

Metal leafing

Metal leaf sheets are very thin squares of metal (real gold or imitation) that are applied to a surface. Metal leafing is also available in silver, copper, and variegated colors.

Metal leaf adhesive

Leaf adhesive holds the leaf to the surface. Follow the adhesive manufacturer's instructions regarding drying times. The adhesive should be slightly tacky to the touch when the leafing is applied.

Pencil with eraser

Use a pencil with a new, flat eraser to left sheets of leafing.

Brushes

Use a foam brush for base painting and for applying leaf adhesive. Use a very soft bristle brush (3/4" or #12 flat) to smooth the leafed surface and brush away crumbs of leafing. A powder makeup brush is perfect for this.

Here's How

1. Paint area to be leafed with dark red paint. Let dry.

2. Brush leaf adhesive over area and let dry, following manufacturer's instructions.

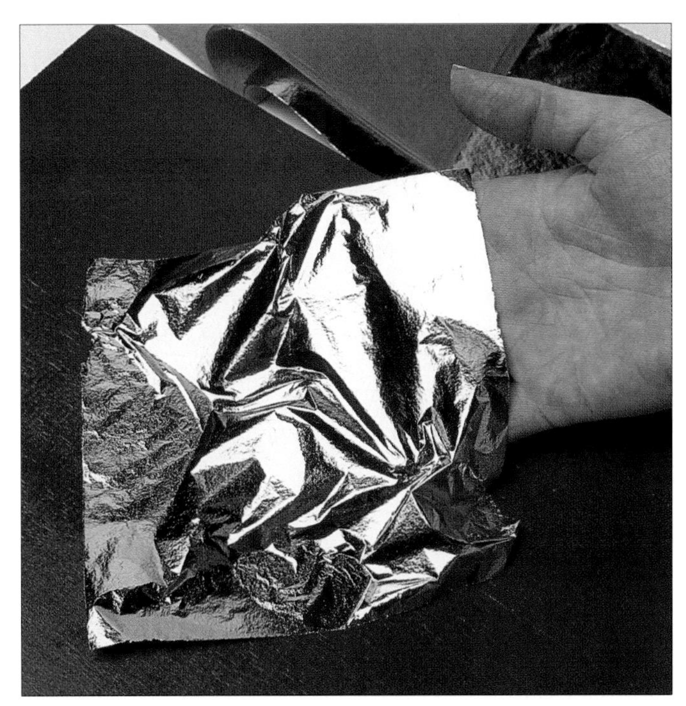

3. Apply sheets of leafing to cover adhesive, one sheet at a time. To pick up leafing sheets, use the eraser end of a pencil after moistening the eraser by touching it to a damp (not wet) cloth. It is almost like "floating" the leafing onto the surface. Lightly press the leafing on the surface, using the soft brush. Repeat, overlapping each piece, until the surface is covered. It is okay if you have wrinkles – they can be patted flat and they only add charm to the piece. It is also okay if you have some areas where the paint shows – this adds a beautifully-worn look to the piece.

4. Pounce surface lightly with a soft brush to smooth. Brush away bits of the leaf. You can further rub the piece with a very soft cloth, such as a piece of velvet to further smooth the piece.

Optional Antiquing: *If the gold looks too garish for you or if your piece has a lot of dimension and carved areas, you may want to add antiquing to the piece. Simply brush antiquing on your piece, a small area at a time. Use a soft cloth to wipe off the desired amount of antiquing. Continue until you have antiqued the entire piece.* ❑

Sponging

Sponging – creating a texture or pattern on a surface with a sponge – can be done randomly for a textured look or with sponge shapes to create a pattern. Variations in the sponge create variations in the effect.

Basic Supplies

Sponges

Natural sea sponges are most often used for textures; cellulose kitchen sponges can be easily cut with scissors to make shapes for sponged patterns. You can also tear the edges of a cellulose sponge to create an irregular shape that can be used for sponging textures. Both types of sponges may be purchased attached to mitts. Find them at hardware and crafts stores.

Paint

Use latex paint (for larger areas) or acrylic craft paint (for smaller projects.) You'll need two (or more) colors. To create transparent sponged effects, mix the paint you're using for sponging with an equal amount of neutral glazing medium.

Palette

Pouring paint for sponging on a paint tray or disposable foam or plastic plates to act as a palette makes it easier to load the sponge.

Here's How

1. Base paint the surface. Let dry.
2. Dampen sponge. Squeeze out excess water. Blot sponge on a towel. The sponge should be damp and pliable, but not wet.
3. Pour paint for sponging on a plate or into a paint tray. Press sponge into paint to load. Blot the loaded sponge on a clean disposable plate or a clean part of the paint tray to distribute the paint.
4. Pounce the sponge on the surface, slightly overlapping each application to create texture.

Sponging Tips

- To make crisp impressions, don't rub or drag the sponge.
- To keep sponging from getting too dense, don't overwork the surface – pounce and move on.
- To avoid a repeated texture, change the position of your hand so you don't have the sponge in the same position every time you touch the surface.

Staining

Staining imparts vibrant hues to wood while allowing the grain and natural characteristics of the wood to show through. The technique can be used to create designs or to create backgrounds for stained, stenciled, stamped, or painted designs. You can also use stain to mellow the look of a painted design by applying it over the design. Simply brush on the stain and wipe away the excess – that's it.

Basic Supplies

Stain

Stains are available in a wide variety of pre-mixed wood tones and colors. It is easy to create your own custom colors by mixing **neutral glazing medium*** with acrylic craft paint, latex paint, or paint glaze.

Options:

- Acrylic paint, latex paint, or paint glaze mixed with neutral glazing medium. The proportions of paint to glazing medium are a matter of personal preference. If you want a more transparent stain, use more glazing medium than paint. (Try two parts glazing medium to one part paint.) If you want a more opaque stain, use more paint and less glazing medium.
- Acrylic stain, available in a variety of pre-mixed shades
- Oil-based stain, available in a variety of pre-mixed shades.

Brushes

Use a sponge brush or a bristle brush to apply stain.

Rags

Use soft, lint-free cloth rags to wipe away excess stain and buff surfaces.

Designs

Use stencils, masking tape, or self-adhesive (contact-type) paper to create designs on surfaces with stain.

**Neutral glazing medium is a clear liquid sold where faux finishing supplies are found.*

Here's How

The technique shown in the photos uses two colors of stain to create a design that resembles parquet.

1. Stain the piece with the lightest color first.

2. Position designs by taping off or using a stencil. Here, self-adhesive paper was applied to the entire surface. The design was transferred to the paper, and areas where the darker stain would be used to create the design were cut away.

3. Stain with the darker color. Peeling away the paper reveals the two stain colors. ❑

Stamping

Stamping is a quick, easy way to create repeated motifs or a handpainted look. Acrylic craft paint or colored paint glaze, a translucent medium with a gel-like consistency, can be used for stamping. It's a good idea to practice stamping on a piece of poster board or paper before stamping your project.

Basic Supplies

Stamps

Stamping can be done with rubber stamps, pre-cut foam stamps, or printing blocks, which come in a wide variety of designs and sizes. You can also cut your own stamps from wood, vegetables, sponges, or dense foam stamp material or use pencil erasers or the wooden ends of brush handles for stamping.

Paint

Use acrylic craft paint or colored paint glaze for all types of stamping. Stamping ink can be used with rubber stamps.

Brushes

Use foam brushes or foam wedges for loading rubber stamps and foam stamps with paint. Use a flat bristle brush for loading printing blocks with paint.

Rubber Stamps: Here's How

1. Load stamp with paint, using a brush. Be careful not to get paint in the crevices of the stamp. Press stamp on surface, being careful not to slide the stamp.

2. Lift the stamp to reveal the image.

Foam Stamps: Here's How

1. Load a foam stamp with paint, using a foam brush.

2. Press the stamp to the surface.

Printing Blocks: Here's How

1. Use a flat bristle brush for loading paint; blend with the brush on the stamp before stamping.

2. Lift the printing block by the handle to reveal the image.

Stenciling

Stenciling is a centuries-old decorative technique for adding painted designs to surfaces in which paint is applied through the cutout areas of a paint-resistant material.

Basic Supplies

Stencils

Stencils are available at crafts and home improvement stores in a huge array of pre-cut designs. You can also buy stencil blank material and cut your own stencils with a craft knife.

Paint

A variety of paints can be used for stenciling, including acrylic craft paint, spray paint, stencil gels (gel-like paints that produce a transparent, watercolor look), and cream stencil paints.

Applicators

The paints can be applied with stencil brushes, small paint rollers, or sponging brushes (round foam sponges on a handle). It's good to have several sizes of brushes – the size of the brush to use is determined by the size of the stencil opening.

Palette

Squeeze puddles of paint on a palette or a disposable foam or plastic plate for loading brushes and applicators.

Here's How

1. Pour some paint on a plate or palette. Holding the stencil brush perpendicular to the plate, dip the tips of the bristles in paint.

2. Lightly pounce the brush on a paper towel to remove excess paint.

3. One way to apply paint through the openings of the stencil is to move the brush in a circular motion, known as the sweeping stroke. Use more pressure to create a darker print.

4. Another way to apply paint to the surface is by pouncing the brush up and down. ❑

Furniture Projects

Many types and styles of furniture – old and new and in-between, fanciful and formal, large and small – are represented in these projects. They are organized according to the type of furniture piece used as the surface:

- Chairs & Stools
- Tables
- Chests of Drawers
- Cabinets
- Kids' Furniture

Create them as they are presented or use the ideas, techniques, and motifs to create your own one-of-a-kind treasures, choosing furniture pieces and colors that suit your decor and color schemes. The finished results will express your style, enliven your rooms, and earn admiration and compliments from your family and friends.

Chairs

Chairs are versatile, useful, portable, and inexpensive. Wooden chairs have a place in every room – even the bathroom. I have a wonderful painted wooden chair in my bathroom that holds a stack of towels. I always need one in my bedroom so I can sit down and tie my shoes. In a dining room, mismatched and painted chairs add a homey cottage look to your décor. A decorative wooden chair in the living room can be pressed into service for extra seating and moved around the room for versatility.

Old wooden chairs are easy to find and are relatively inexpensive. If they need repairing, most times they are easy to repair by adding a little wood glue to the joints to stabilize them. Unfinished wooden chairs can be found in quite a variety of styles.

The seven projects in this section can be used to add color and visual interest to all kinds of rooms.

Pictured opposite: *Blue Flower & Butterflies Ladderback Chair. Instructions begin on page 40.*

BLUE FLOWER & BUTTERFLIES

ladderback chair

This ladderback chair is adorned with butterflies and decorated with stripes, dots, squiggles, and sponging reminiscent of painted Easter eggs. The divisions of the rush seat form the petals of a giant blue flower.

Created by Holly Buttimer

Techniques Used: Decorative painting, sponging

SUPPLIES

Surface:
Wooden ladderback chair with rush seat

Acrylic Craft Paint:
Black
Dark green
Lemonade
Limeade
Metallic blue
Metallic gold
Metallic periwinkle
Metallic purple
Metallic silver
Olive
Orange
Pastel green
Periwinkle
Royal blue
White
Yellow

Other supplies:
Flat and round bristle brushes in a variety of sizes
Tracing paper & pencil
Transfer paper & stylus
Small sea sponge
Gloss sealer spray

INSTRUCTIONS

Prepare:
Prepare chair for painting, following the instructions in the "Preparation" section.

Base Paint:
1. Base paint wooden parts of chair with periwinkle and limeade, using photo as a guide for color placement.
2. Base paint seat with periwinkle. Let dry.
3. Trace and transfer patterns for flower to chair seat and butterflies to chair back.

Paint Blue Butterflies:
The blue butterflies are painted on the limeade sections.
1. Paint wings with periwinkle.
2. Darken near body with metallic periwinkle.
3. Outline with royal blue.
4. Highlight edges with white.
5. Paint body and antennae with black. Highlight with gold bands.

Paint Green Butterflies:
The green butterflies are painted on the periwinkle sections.
1. Paint wings with limeade.
2. Darken near body with olive.
3. Highlight edges and paint body with white.
4. Outline butterflies and paint antennae with black.
5. Highlight body with lemonade.

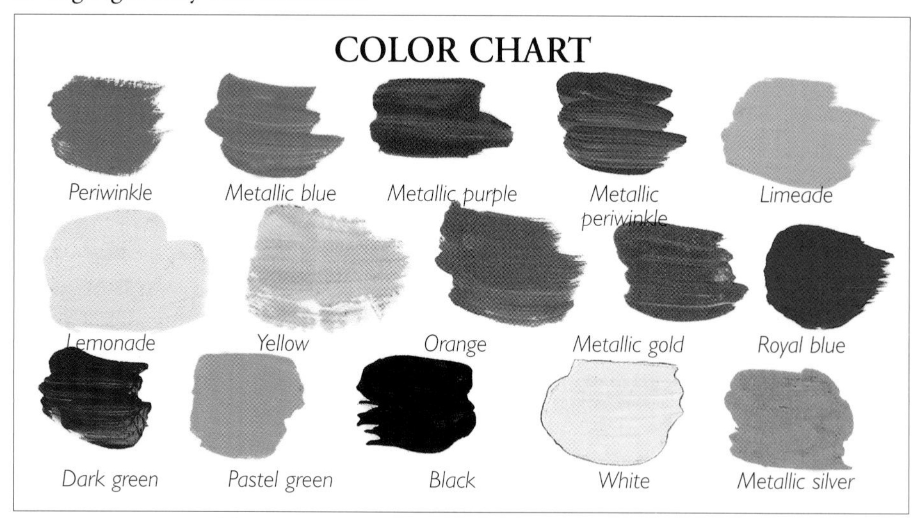

Paint Flower:
1. Paint petals with metallic periwinkle. Streak with metallic blue and royal blue.
2. Paint center, using photo as a guide, with periwinkle, then limeade, then orange, then lemonade. Streak with lemonade area with yellow.
3. Paint leaves with limeade. Shade with pastel green + olive.
4. Add outlines and details with black.

Decorate:
1. Add horizontal lines, wavy lines, vertical lines, and dab dots to back of chair and front legs, using photo as a guide. Use metallic periwinkle on limeade areas and limeade on periwinkle areas for contrast.
2. Paint stretchers with metallic silver and metallic gold.
3. Paint bands between sections with metallic gold and metallic silver.
4. Dampen a sea sponge. Squeeze out excess water. Sponge silver areas with gold and gold areas with silver.
5. Paint finials at top of back with gold. Let dry.
6. Dampen the sea sponge. Squeeze out excess water. Sponge finials with silver.
7. Sponge the back legs with metallic gold, metallic silver, and metallic periwinkle. Let dry.

Finish:
Spray with several coats gloss sealer. Let dry between coats. ❑

Blue butterfly

Green butterfly

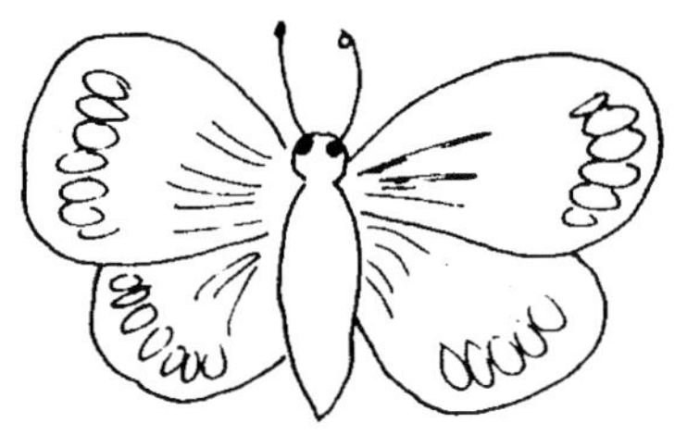

Patterns for Blue Flower & Butterflies

Enlarge @165% for actual size.

Flower: Draw four petals and four leaves to complete pattern.

BUNNY & DAFFODILS

wooden chair

The bunny design was painted directly on the old leatherette seat of this chair, and the carved flower design at the middle back was painted in vibrant colors. Ball trim can be added to ornament the back.

Created by Holly Buttimer

Techniques Used: Decorative painting, sponging

SUPPLIES

Surface:
Wooden chair

Acrylic Craft Paint:
Black
Blue
Burgundy
Cinnamon
Dark green
Leaf green
Lemonade
Limelight
Metallic copper
Metallic gold
Metallic peach
Metallic purple
Orange
Violet
White
Yellow

Other Supplies:
Tracing paper & pencil
Transfer paper & stylus
Multi-purpose comb
Neutral glazing medium
Artist's paint brushes – flats, rounds, and liners of various sizes
Small sea sponge
3 wooden balls
Finishing nails and wood glue
Waterbase varnish, gloss sheen

INSTRUCTIONS

Prepare:
Prepare chair for painting, following instructions in the "Preparation" section.

Paint & Comb Legs & Sides:
1. Base paint with limelight. Let dry.
2. Mix two parts dark green paint and one part neutral glazing medium. Working one section at a time, brush glaze mixture over legs and sides. While glaze is still wet, work comb through glaze, removing some of the glaze to create texture. Continue until all sections are complete. Let dry overnight.

Paint Upper Back & Apron:
1. Paint upper part of back and apron with blue. Let dry.
2. Trace and transfer carrot pattern.
3. Paint carrots with orange. Shade with cinnamon and metallic copper. Highlight with yellow and metallic gold.
4. Paint carrot tops with green. Shade with dark green. Highlight with limeade.
5. Outline and add details with black.

Continued on page 44

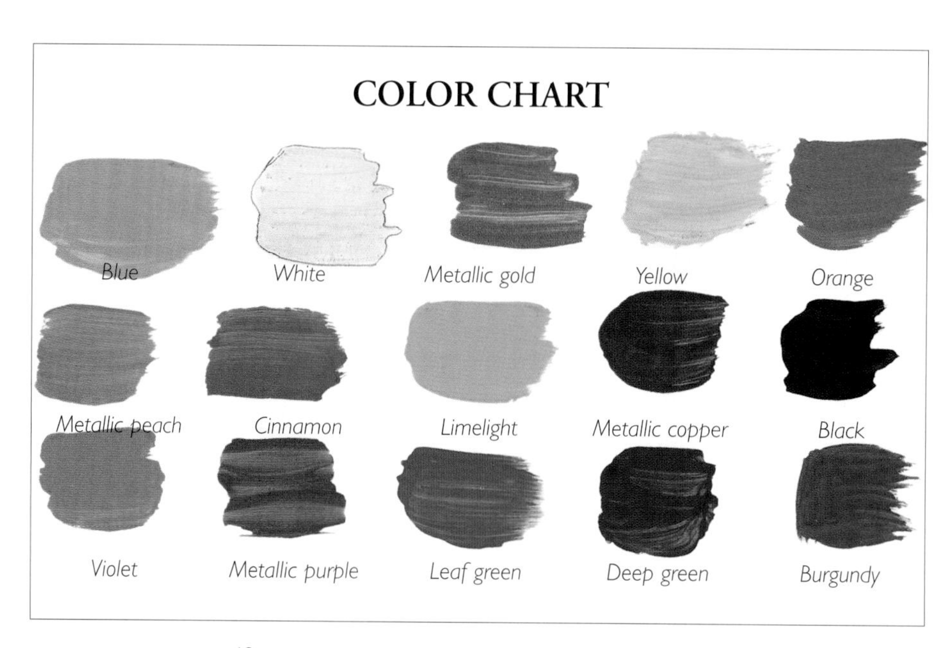

continued from page 42

Paint Middle Back & Ball Trim:

If your chair has a carved flower, you can paint the carving as was done here. If not, trace and transfer the flower pattern.

1. Paint petals with metallic purple. Streak with violet.
2. Paint center with white. Dab with yellow.
3. Highlight center and petals with metallic gold.
4. Paint leaves with leaf green. Shade with dark green. Highlight with limelight.
5. Paint remainder of back piece with alternating stripes of black and metallic copper.
6. Paint ball trim with orange. Let dry. Sponge with copper metallic.

Paint Seat:

1. Base paint with blue. Let dry.
2. Trace and transfer the design.
3. Paint bunny's fur with white. Shade with metallic purple. Highlight with metallic gold.
4. Paint iris of eye with cinnamon. Highlight with metallic gold and metallic copper. Paint pupil with black. Highlight with white.
5. Paint inner ears and nose with cinnamon. Highlight with metallic peach.
6. Paint grass with streaks of leaf green, limelight, and dark green. Use same colors to paint daffodil leaves and stems.
7. Paint daffodils with yellow. Streak with gold. Highlight with lemonade. Shade with violet.
8. Outline flowers and rabbit with black.
9. Streak sky with white. Let dry.

Finish:

1. Attach ball trim to back of chair with finishing nails and glue. Let dry.
2. Apply several coats gloss varnish to seal. Let dry between coats. ❑

Patterns for Bunny & Daffodils

Chair Back – Enlarge @150% for actual size.

Pattern for Bunny & Daffodils

Chair Seat – Enlarge @145% for actual size

BUNNY IN THE MEADOW

wooden stool

Crackling provides texture to the background of this simple wooden stool. Combed designs on the seat edge and legs and metallic-painted accents provide more texture and interest.

Created by Holly Buttimer

Techniques Used: Decorative painting, crackling, sponging

SUPPLIES

Surface:
Wooden stool

Acrylic Craft Paint:
Black
Blue
Burgundy
Cinnamon
Dark green
Leaf green
Limelight
Metallic copper
Metallic gold
Metallic peach
Metallic purple
Orange
Violet
White
Yellow

Other Supplies:
Tracing paper & pencil
Transfer paper & stylus
Multi-purpose comb
Neutral glazing medium
Crackle medium
Artist's paint brushes – flats, rounds, and liners of various sizes
Small sea sponge
Waterbase varnish, gloss sheen

INSTRUCTIONS

Prepare:
Prepare stool for painting, following instructions in the "Preparation" section.

Paint Legs:
1. Paint legs with burgundy. Let dry.
2. Paint leg stretchers with limelight. Let dry.
3. Mix two parts dark green paint and one part neutral glazing medium. Working one section at a time, brush glaze mixture over stretchers. While glaze is still wet, comb through glaze to create stripes, removing some of the glaze. Clean comb by wiping periodically with a rag. Continue until all stretchers are complete. Reserve remaining glaze. Let dry overnight.

Paint, Crackle & Comb Seat:
1. Base paint seat with metallic purple. Let dry.
2. Brush seat with crackle medium, following instructions for "Crackling" in the "Techniques" section.
3. Brush over crackle medium with violet. Cracks will form. Let dry completely.
4. Paint edges of seat with limelight. Let dry.
5. Brush reserved dark green glaze over paint, one area at a time. While glaze is still wet, comb through glaze to create a wavy pattern, removing some of the glaze. Wipe comb on rags periodically. Continue until complete. Let dry overnight. *Tip:* Use a damp rag to remove any glaze that gets on the crackled center section.

Paint Design on Seat:
1. Trace and transfer the design.
2. Paint rabbit's fur with white. Shade with metallic purple. Highlight with metallic gold.
3. Paint iris of eye with cinnamon. Highlight with metallic gold and metallic copper. Paint pupil with black. Highlight with white.
4. Paint inner ears and nose with cinnamon. Highlight with metallic peach.
5. Paint grass with streaks of leaf green, limelight, yellow, and dark green.
6. Paint daisy petals with white. Paint centers with yellow and orange. Highlight petals with copper and cinnamon. Let dry.
7. Paint pansy petals with yellow and metallic purple. Paint centers with two dabs of white and one dab of leaf green.
8. Outline flowers and rabbit with black.

Finish:
1. Paint a thin band of metallic copper around edge of rabbit design on seat. Let dry.
2. Apply several coats gloss varnish to seal. Let dry between coats. ❑

Pattern for Bunny in the Meadow Wooden Stool

Enlarge @140% for actual size.

Actual Size Pattern for Summer Garden Wooden Chair

Instructions on page 51

See placement diagram following instructions for position of design elements.

SUMMER GARDEN

wooden chair

Flowers in full bloom and ripe fruits, plus butterflies, a dragonfly, and a bee, celebrate the lush bounty of the summer garden all year long.

Created by Holly Buttimer

Techniques Used: Decorative painting, sponging

SUPPLIES

Surface:
Wooden chair

Acrylic Craft Paint:
Black
Blue
Chocolate brown
Dark green
Fuchsia
Lavender
Leaf green
Lemonade
Light brown
Limelight
Magenta
Metallic gold
Ochre
Orange
Pink
White
Wild iris
Wine
Yellow

Other Supplies:
Small cellulose sponge
Sponge brushes
Artist's paint brushes – flats, rounds, and liners of various sizes
Waterbase varnish

INSTRUCTIONS

Prepare:
Prepare chair for painting, following instructions in the "Preparation" section.

Base Paint:
Use the photo as a guide for color placement, adapting the designs to fit your chair.

1. Transfer the outline of the seat design to the chair. Base paint inner area with blue. Base paint outer area and top of upper back slat with lemonade.
2. Base paint front legs, sides of back legs, and back slats with blue.
3. Base paint leg stretchers, fronts of back legs, the ball trim, and the edges of the seat with lavender.
4. Base paint the apron with leaf green. While paint is still wet, add horizontal streaks of limelight, blending slightly. Let dry.

Continued on next page

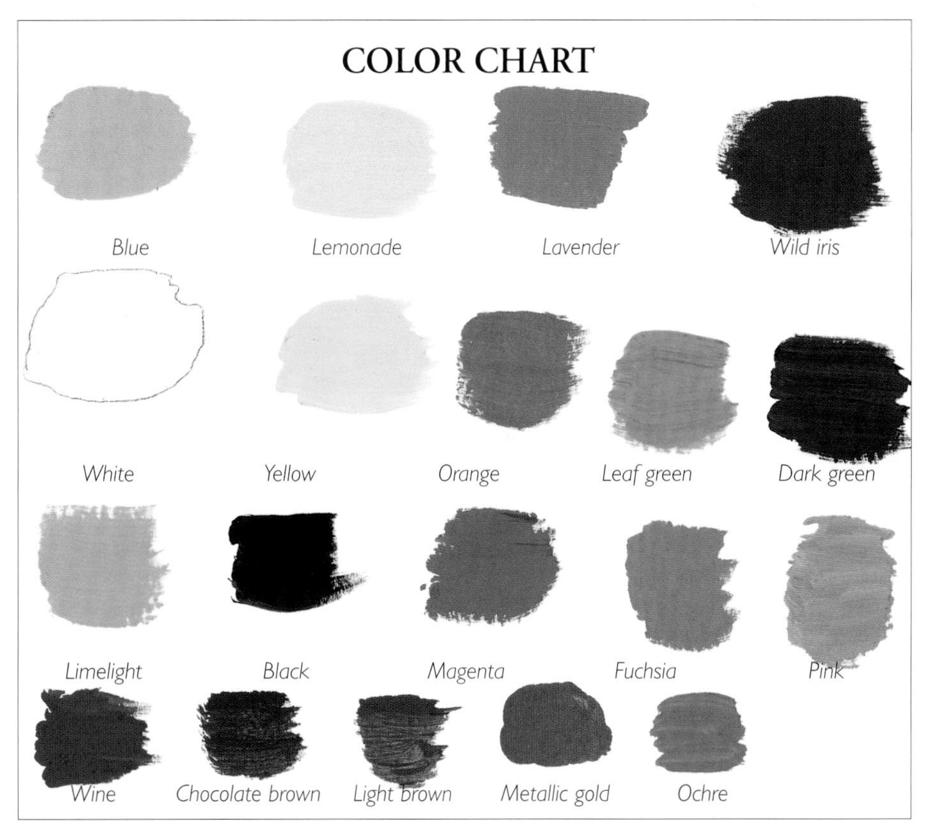

continued from page 51

Paint the Back Designs:

1. Transfer patterns for pansies and butterfly to back slats.
2. Paint the pansy petals with lavender and wild iris. Shade with black. Highlight with white.
3. Paint the centers with yellow and orange. Accent with black.
4. Paint leaves with leaf green. Shade with dark green. Highlight with limelight. Outline with black.
5. Paint the butterfly's wings with limelight, lavender, and fuchsia. Paint body with orange. Highlight with pink. Shade with magenta.
6. Add details, antennae, and outlines to butterfly with black.

Paint the Seat Design:

The instructions begin with the butterfly at the center back of the seat and continue clockwise around the seat.

1. Transfer design to seat.
2. Butterfly at back – Paint wings with lavender, wild iris, fuchsia, pink, and yellow. Add details and outlines and paint body with black. Streak and highlight with light brown and metallic gold.
3. Bee – Paint body with yellow and black. Highlight with lemonade. Shade with ochre. Paint wings with white. Shade with blue. Highlight with metallic gold.
4. Five-petal flowers – Paint three petals with white, using photo as a guide for placement. Paint two petals with wild iris. Paint center with yellow, then orange. Streak petals with lavender and blue.
5. Apples – Paint with red. Shade with chocolate brown and wine. Add dots with brown. Highlight with orange and yellow. Paint stems and tendrils with light brown. Shade with black. Highlight with metallic gold.
6. Strawberries – Paint with red. Highlight with fuchsia and yellow. Shade with wine and chocolate brown. Paint seeds with black. Highlight with white.
7. Flower with buds – Paint petals with white. Add streaks of wild iris and blue. Paint center with yellow, then orange, then black. Highlight with metallic gold. Outline and add details with black.
8. Cherries – Paint with red. Shade with chocolate brown and wine. Highlight with orange and yellow. Paint stems and tendrils with light brown. Shade with black. Highlight with metallic gold.
9. Dragonfly – Paint body with leaf green. Shade with wild iris. Highlight with limelight, then pink and blue. Paint wings with white. Highlight with pink, blue, and limelight.
10. Butterfly at center – Paint wings with black, yellow, orange, and lemonade, using photo as a guide for placement. Highlight with white, ochre, and metallic gold. Add details with black.
11. Daisies – Paint petals with white. Shade with blue. Paint centers with yellow. Accent with orange and light brown. Outline petals with black.
12. Leaves & stems – Paint leaves with leaf green. Shade with dark green. Highlight with limelight. Outline with black.

Paint the Apron Design:

1. Paint daisy petals with white.
2. Paint centers with yellow. Highlight at top with lemonade. Shade at bottom with orange.

Decorate:

1. Sponge leg stretchers, fronts of back legs, the ball trim, and the edges of the seat randomly with limelight.
2. Sponge ball trim and top edge of upper back slat with limelight.
3. Paint freehand stripes on front legs and sides of back legs with lemonade. Add dots on lower back slat with lemonade.
4. Paint circle outline on seat with light brown. Highlight with metallic gold. Let dry.

Finish:

Apply several coats of waterbase varnish to protect the painted design. Let dry between coats. ❑

Placement Diagram

for Summer Garden Wooden Chair

Actual Size Patterns for Summer Garden Wooden Chair

See placement diagram for position of design elements.

Patterns for Summer Garden

Corner and Front of Seat – Actual Size Pattern

Chair Back

Chair Seat – Actual Size Pattern
See placement diagram for position of design elements.

Enlarge @110% for actual size.

Patterns for Beautiful Butterfly Painted Pillow

Instructions on page 56

Enlarge @115% for actual size.

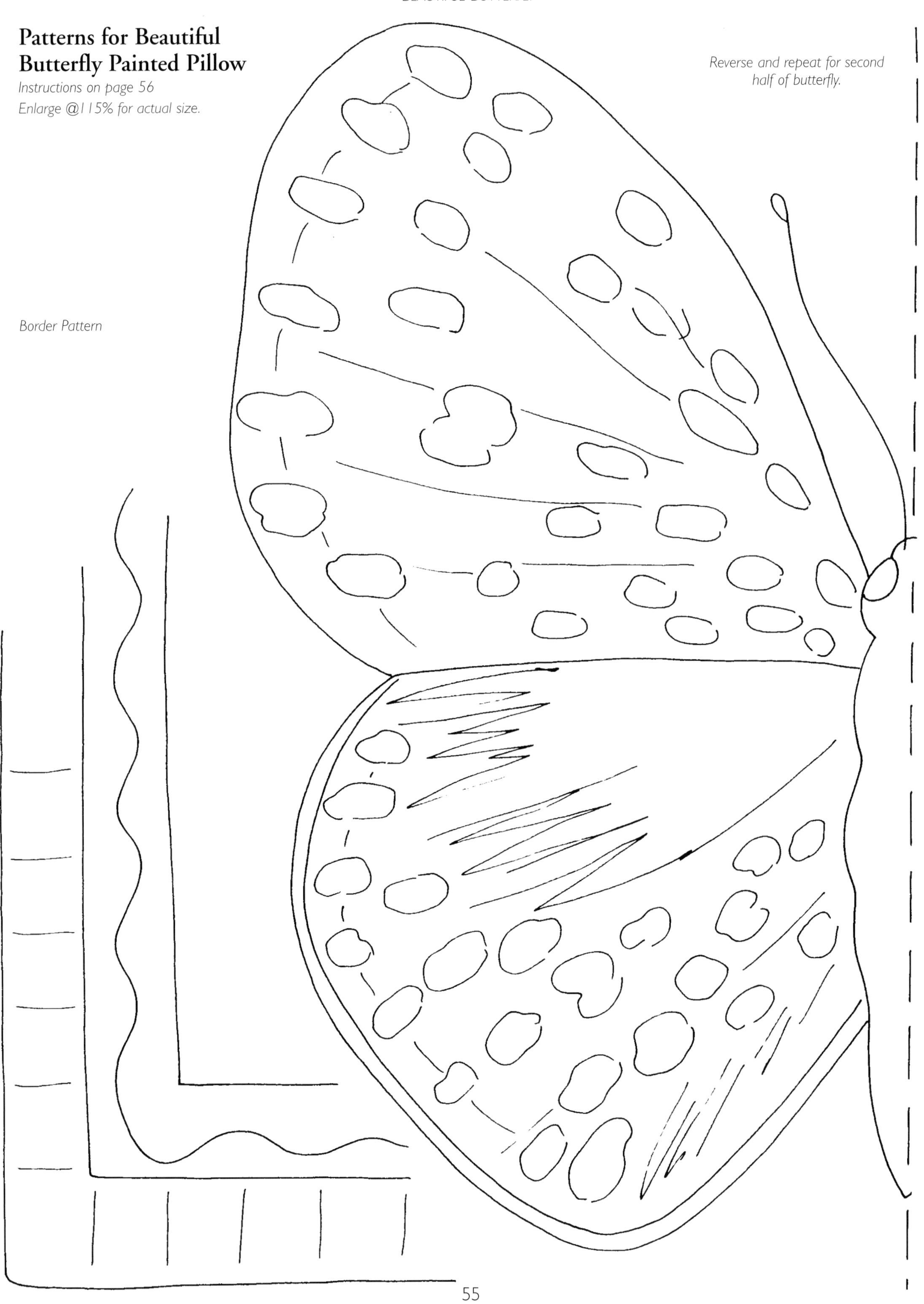

BEAUTIFUL BUTTERFLY

painted pillow

Paint a pillow to accent and add color to a chair or a bench. Painted fabrics are a great way to create a one-of-a-kind look. Paint one to match your chair.

Created by Holly Buttimer

Techniques Used: Decorative painting

SUPPLIES

Surface:

Lightweight canvas fabric, size for desired pillow

Acrylic Craft Paint:

Black
Lemonade
Metallic blue
Metallic copper
Metallic gold
Metallic periwinkle
Ochre
White

Other Supplies:

Artist's paint brushes – flats of various sizes and liners
Transfer paper & stylus
Textile medium
Iron & pressing cloth
Pillow form, zipper, thread

INSTRUCTIONS

Prepare:

1. Wash and dry fabric. **Don't** use a fabric softener. Press. Cut to size.
2. Transfer pattern to fabric.
3. Mix acrylic paints with textile medium according to textile medium manufacturer's instructions.

Paint the Design:

Work on a sturdy surface covered with plastic and blank newsprint or absorbent paper.

1. Paint the butterfly with black.
2. Streak wings with metallic gold and metallic copper.
3. Dot wings with metallic blue and metallic periwinkle.
4. Outline, add lines on wings, highlight body, and paint eyes with metallic gold.
5. Streak the background with lemonade, metallic gold, and ochre.
6. Paint inner border with metallic periwinkle.
7. Paint outer border with metallic gold.
8. Paint stripes on gold border and outline borders with black. Let cure 24 hours.

Finish:

1. Heat set painted design. To heat set, place pressing cloth over the painted design and press at the highest heat setting appropriate for the fabric. Hold the iron on the covered area for 30 seconds. Repeat until all areas have been heat set. Let cool. Don't wash for 72 hours.
2. Stitch zipper in back. Stitch pillow front to pillow back, right sides together. Turn pillow and insert pillow form. ❑

NORTH AMERICAN TREES

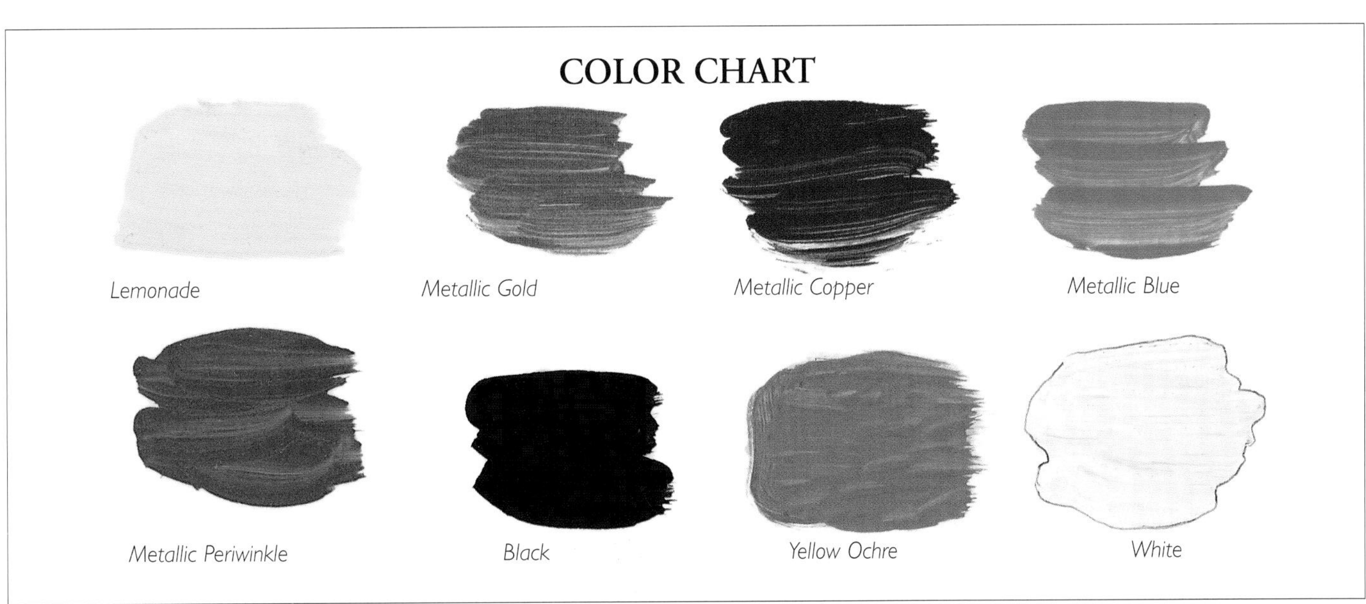
COLOR CHART
Lemonade
Metallic Gold
Metallic Copper
Metallic Blue
Metallic Periwinkle
Black
Yellow Ochre
White

GO FISH

wooden chair

Fish motifs cut from wrapping paper adorn this chair that's painted with colors to match the paper motifs. The stamped dot trim echoes the air bubbles from the printed paper.

Created by Kathi Malarchuk Bailey

Techniques Used: Decoupage, distressing, sponging, stamping

Surface:
Wooden chair

Paint:
Light blue latex paint, eggshell or satin finish
Acrylic craft paints, 2 oz. bottles – bright blue, purple, white
Neutral glazing medium, 4 oz.

Other Supplies:
Fish design wrapping paper
Decoupage finish
Small cellulose sponge
Sandpaper
Tack cloth
Masking tape
Foam brushes
Scissors
Foam plates (for palette)

INSTRUCTIONS

Prepare:
Clean and prepare chair for painting as needed, following instructions in the "Preparation" section.

Paint & Sponge & Stamp:
1. Base paint entire chair with two coats of light blue latex paint. Let dry and sand between coats.
2. To antique, mix one part bright blue acrylic paint with three parts neutral glazing medium. Be sure mixture is blended thoroughly. Dampen cellulose sponge and dip into glaze mixture. Wipe horizontally over chair back and seat. Wipe vertically down legs and back rails. Do not over-wipe, as you may remove glaze. Let dry overnight.
3. Mask off around top of chair back and seat trim. Paint trim with two coats purple acrylic paint. Remove tape. Let dry.
4. Create dots by dipping the wooden end of a foam brush in white acrylic paint. Stamp dots around edge of seat and top of chair back.
5. Distress entire chair slightly by sanding lightly. Wipe with tack cloth.

Decoupage & Finish:
1. Cut out fish motifs and air bubbles from paper with scissors. Coat backs of cutouts with decoupage finish. Adhere to seat and top of chair back. Let dry according to manufacturer's instructions.
2. Seal entire chair with two coats of decoupage finish. ❑

COFFEE BREAK

spindle-back chair

A riot of color and textures enliven this wooden chair. The turned legs and back are embellished with metallic paint.

Created by Holly Buttimer

Techniques Used: Decorative painting, sponging

SUPPLIES

Surface:
Wooden spindle-back chair

Acrylic Craft Paint:
Black
Blue
Chocolate brown
Copper
Dark green
Fuchsia
Gray
Leaf green
Lemonade
Light periwinkle
Lime
Magenta
Metallic champagne
Metallic gold
Metallic peach
Nutmeg
Ochre
Periwinkle
Pink
Red
White
Yellow

Other Supplies:
Cellulose sponge
Sponge brushes
Artist's paint brushes – flats, rounds, and liners of various sizes
Waterbase varnish

INSTRUCTIONS

Prepare:

1. Clean and prepare chair for painting as needed, following instructions in the "Preparation" section.
2. Transfer the patterns to the chair seat and back.

Paint the Seat Design:

1. Paint the background areas with periwinkle.
2. Paint the tablecloth with red. Add spirals with black.
3. Paint coffee cup and vase with yellow. Highlight with lemonade. Shade with ochre.
4. Decorate coffee cup with periwinkle. Paint handles of vase with periwinkle. Highlight with light periwinkle.
5. Paint coffee in cup with nutmeg. Shade with chocolate brown. Highlight with white.
6. Paint steam rising from coffee with white. Highlight with metallic champagne and metallic gold.

Continued on next page

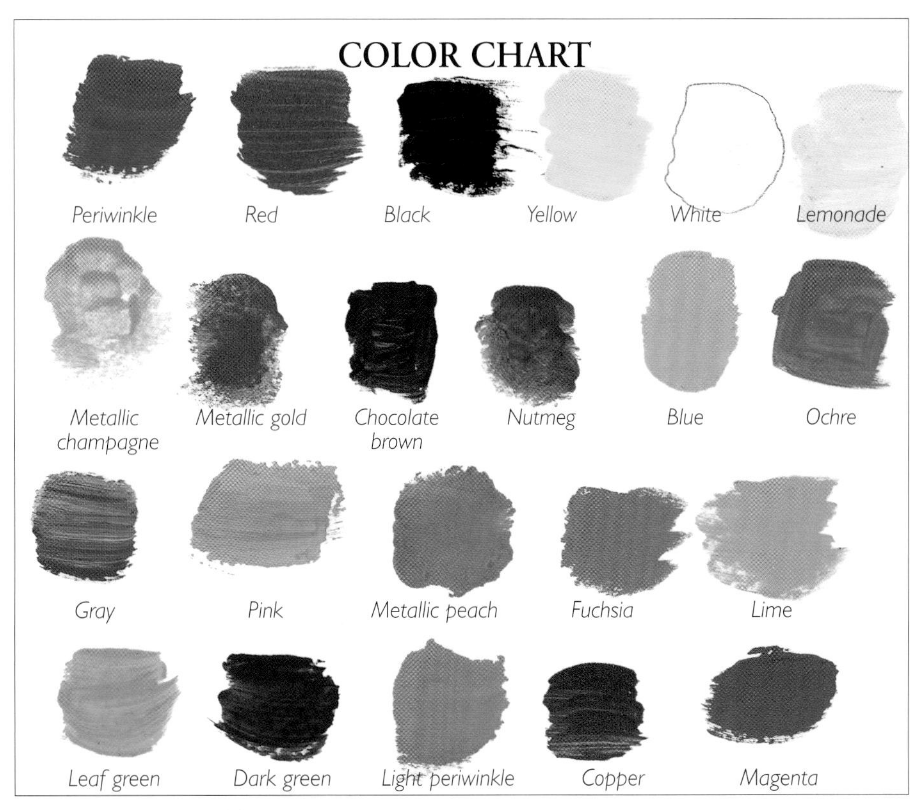

continued from page 61

7. Paint spoon with gray. Shade with black. Highlight with white.
8. Paint chair seat with yellow. Highlight with lemonade. Shade with ochre.
9. Paint stripes on seat with periwinkle.
10. Paint chair back with black. Highlight with metallic champagne and white.
11. Paint cupcake plate with white. Accent with blue.
12. Paint cupcake cups with gray. Add details with black.
13. Paint cupcake frosting with white. Accent with pink. Paint cherries with pink. Highlight with white.
14. Paint yellow roses with yellow. Shade with ochre. Highlight with lemonade. Accent with metallic peach and metallic gold.
15. Paint red roses with red. Shade with magenta. Highlight with pink.
16. Paint pink roses with pink. Shade with fuchsia. Highlight with metallic peach and white.
17. Paint centers with black and outline roses with black. Add dabs of lime at the centers.
18. Paint leaves with leaf green. Shade with dark green. Highlight with lime, lemonade, and white. Outline with black.

Decorate the Rest of the Chair:

Adapt these ideas to suit your chair.

1. Transfer the pattern to the top back of the chair.
2. Paint rose with pink. Shade with magenta. Highlight with lemonade.
3. Paint rose center with black. Add dabs of lime.
4. Paint top scroll design with dark green. Add stripes with leaf green, lime, lemonade, and white.
5. Paint area below scrolls with light periwinkle. Add streaks of periwinkle and metallic gold.
6. Paint alternating spindles with lemonade and red. Sponge red spindles with metallic gold. Sponge lemonade spindles with metallic gold and metallic copper.
7. Paint the back supports, leg stretchers, and legs with colors from the seat painting, using the photo as a guide for color placement. Sponge, add dots and stripes, and use metallic colors to create interest. Let dry completely.

Finish:

Apply several coats waterbase varnish. Let dry between coats. ❑

Patterns for Coffee Break Spindle-Back Chair

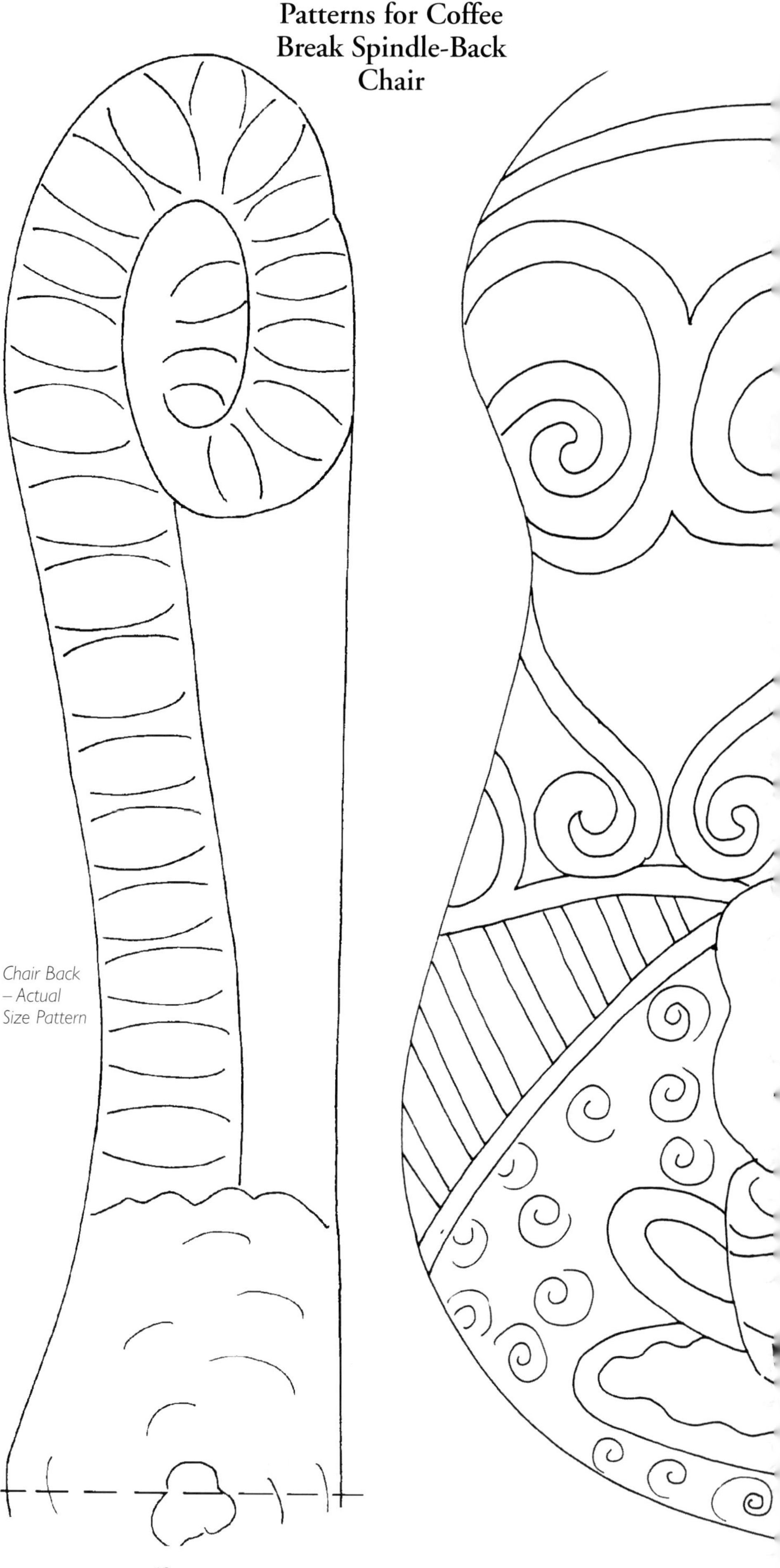

Chair Seat Pattern – Enlarge @ 170% for actual size.

Tables

A table may be the focal point in a dining room breakfast room, or kitchen or an accent piece in a family room, den, or bedroom. So make it special. Tables will allow for lots of decorating space – the top surface is a blank canvas for you to work your decorating wonders. The five projects in this section provide decorating ideas for all kinds of tables – all of them loaded with plenty of style.

Pictured at right: *Flowers, Fruit & Butterflies Round Wooden Table. Instructions* *begin on page 66.*

FLOWERS, FRUIT & BUTTERFLIES

round wooden table

The dark background and metallic accents give an Old World look to this simple round table. How lovely this would be in an entry or as a bedside table.

Created by Holly Buttimer

Techniques Used: Decorative painting

SUPPLIES

Surface:
Round wooden table

Acrylic Craft Paint:
Black
Blue
Chocolate brown
Dark green
Deep charcoal gray
Fuchsia
Lavender
Leaf green
Lemonade
Light brown
Limelight
Magenta
Metallic gold
Ochre
Orange
Pink
Red
White
Wild iris
Wine
Yellow

Other Supplies:
Sponge brushes
Neutral glazing medium
Multi-purpose comb
Cloth rags
Artist's paint brushes – flats, rounds, and liners of various sizes
Pen with gold metallic ink
Spray sealer

INSTRUCTIONS

Prepare:
Prepare table for painting, following instructions in the "Preparation" section.

Base Paint:
1. Paint top with deep charcoal gray.
2. Paint legs with pink.

Comb Legs:
Mix two parts wine paint and one part neutral glazing medium. Working one section at a time, brush glaze mixture over legs. While glaze is still wet, comb through glaze to create stripes, removing some of the glaze. Clean comb by wiping periodically with a rag. Continue until all legs are complete. Let dry overnight.

Paint the Design:
The instructions begin with the apple at the center back and continue clockwise around the tabletop.

1. Transfer design to tabletop.
2. Apple – Paint with red. Shade with chocolate brown and wine. Add dots with brown. Highlight with orange and yellow. Paint stems and tendrils with light brown. Shade with black. Highlight with metallic gold.
3. Calla lily – Paint with lemonade. Shade with ochre and lavender. Highlight with white. Shade center and paint bud with wine. Highlight with white.
4. Purple butterfly – Paint wings with lavender, yellow, ochre, and light brown. Streak lavender areas with white. Paint body and antennae with black. Edge wings with black.
5. Beetle – Paint with black. Streak head with light brown. Streak body with leaf green, lemonade, and metallic gold.
6. Five-petaled flower – Paint with black. Highlight with lavender and white. Paint center with white. Streak with yellow. Add details with metallic gold.
7. Pear – Paint with yellow. Shade with wine. Paint spots and stem with light brown. Highlight with lemonade and gold metallic.
8. Ladybug – Paint body with red and black. Highlight with white.
9. Gold butterfly – Paint wings with yellow and black. Paint body with black. Highlight and streak yellow areas with lemonade and ochre. Highlight black areas with metallic gold. Add detail lines with light brown.
10. Four-petaled flowers – Paint back petals with wild iris. Highlight with white. Paint front petals with white. Shade with gold. Paint center with yellow. Edge with orange.
11. Pink and gold butterfly – Paint wings with white, magenta, and lemonade. Paint body and add wing details with black. Highlight body with white.
12. Bee – Paint body with yellow and black, stippling the head for a fuzzy look. Highlight with lemonade. Shade with ochre. Paint wings with white. Shade with blue. Highlight with metallic gold.

Continued on page 68

Actual Size Patterns

Use photo as a guide for placement of design elements.

Use photo as a guide for placement of design elements.

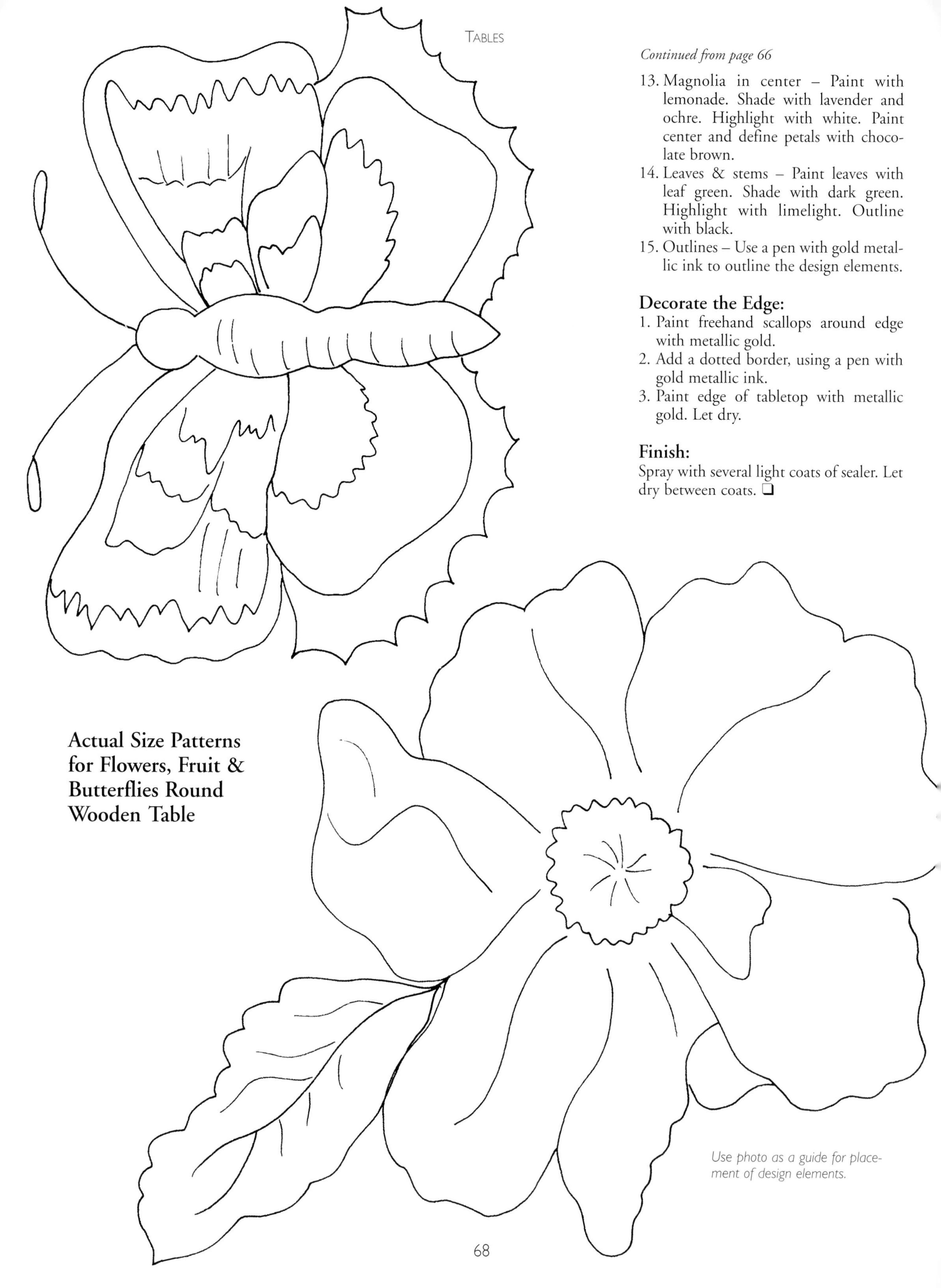

Continued from page 66

13. Magnolia in center – Paint with lemonade. Shade with lavender and ochre. Highlight with white. Paint center and define petals with chocolate brown.
14. Leaves & stems – Paint leaves with leaf green. Shade with dark green. Highlight with limelight. Outline with black.
15. Outlines – Use a pen with gold metallic ink to outline the design elements.

Decorate the Edge:

1. Paint freehand scallops around edge with metallic gold.
2. Add a dotted border, using a pen with gold metallic ink.
3. Paint edge of tabletop with metallic gold. Let dry.

Finish:

Spray with several light coats of sealer. Let dry between coats. ❑

Actual Size Patterns for Flowers, Fruit & Butterflies Round Wooden Table

Use photo as a guide for placement of design elements.

Enlarge @145% for actual size.

DRAGONFLIES IN FLIGHT

wooden console table

Dragonflies in vivid metallic colors adorn the crackled top of this simple console table. This table would look so special behind a comfy sofa in an informal family room.

Created by Kirsten Jones

Techniques Used: Crackling, decorative painting, distressing

SUPPLIES

Surface:
Wooden console table

Acrylic Craft Paint:
Light periwinkle
Lime yellow
Metallic peridot
Metallic periwinkle
Metallic plum
Orchid
Wicker white

Other Supplies:
Tracing paper & pencil
Transfer paper & stylus
Artist's paint brushes – 1" flat, #8 round
Fine tip black permanent marker
Crackle medium
Sandpaper
Tack cloth
Aerosol sealer, gloss sheen

Instructions follow on page 72

continued from page 70

INSTRUCTIONS

Prepare:
Prepare table for painting, following instructions in "Preparation" section.

Base Paint:
1. Paint apron and legs with lime yellow. Let dry.
2. Paint top with wicker white. Let dry.

Crackle:
See instructions in "Decorating Techniques" section for crackling.
1. Brush crackle medium on tabletop. Let dry.
2. Apply Light Periwinkle over crackle medium. Let dry. Cracks will form as the paint dries.

Paint Design:
1. Trace dragonfly pattern and transfer to top of table, positioning motifs as shown in photo.
2. Paint some dragonflies' bodies with peridot, others with orchid.
3. Shade peridot bodies with periwinkle. Shade orchid bodies with plum.
4. Paint wings with a wash of wicker white. Let dry.
5. Streak wings with orchid and periwinkle, using photo as a guide. Let dry.

Finish:
1. Outline and add details with black marker.
2. Distress legs slightly by sanding lightly with sandpaper. Wipe with tack cloth.
3. Spray with several coats gloss sealer. Let dry between coats. ❑

Actual Size Pattern for Dragonflies

CHECKS & STRIPES

wooden end table

This "Early American" style end table is given a fanciful turn with simple handpainted designs and glass drawer pulls. The bright colors are mellowed after painting with an antiquing stain.

Created by Lindsey Mahaffey

Techniques Used: Decorative painting, sponging, staining

SUPPLIES

Surface:
Wooden end table with drawers (This one is 22" x 27", 23" tall.)

Acrylic Craft Paint:
Baby blue
Brown
Charcoal
Lime sherbet
Maroon
Midnight blue
Mustard
Pink
Sage

Artist's Paint Brushes:
1", 1/4" flats
1/4" round
Script liner

Other Supplies:
Neutral glazing medium
Cloth rags
Cellulose sponge
Masking tape
Ruler & pencil
Small sponge
4 glass drawer pulls
Waterbase varnish

INSTRUCTIONS

Prepare:
Remove drawer and drawer pulls. Prepare the table for painting, following instructions in the "Preparation" section.

Base Paint:
1. Base paint the top, the drawer front, and the section with the drawer with two coats mustard. Let dry and sand between coats.
2. Base paint the apron with baby blue. While paint is still wet, wipe gently with a damp rag for a textured, primitive look.
3. Base paint other sections of the table with the paint colors listed above, using the photo as a guide for placement. Mask off sections as needed. Remove all tape and let dry.

Decorate Sides & Back of Drawer Section:
1. Use a 1" flat brush to paint wavy stripes about 2" wide with maroon. Let dry.
2. Paint simple stroke flowers randomly over stripes, using a 1/4" round brush with baby blue and pink for the petals and a smaller round brush with sage for the leaves and centers. See "End Table Painting Guide," Fig. 3.
3. Use a liner brush to line the stripes with tiny dots of midnight blue.

continued on page 76

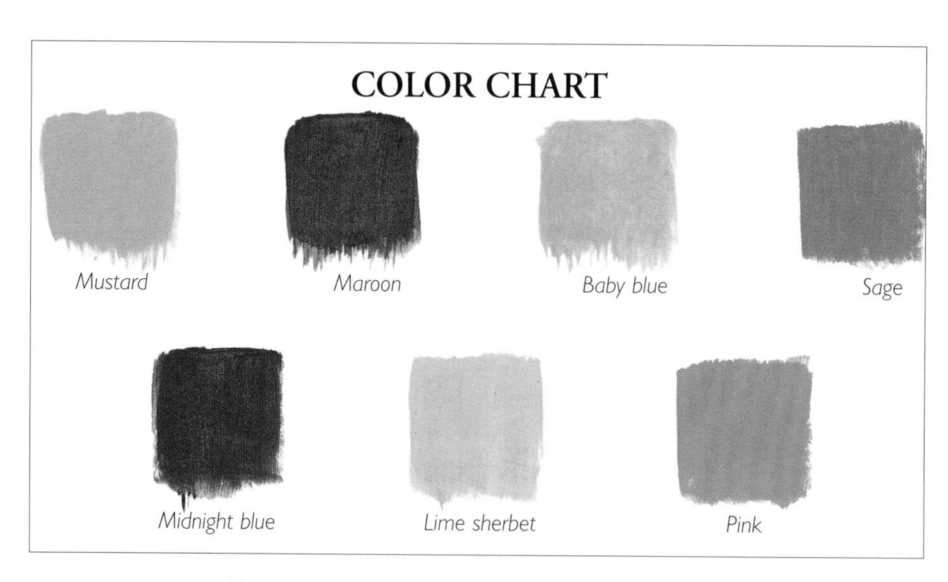

continued from page 74

Decorate the Drawer Front:

1. Use a ruler and pencil to measure and mark checks 3/8" square on the drawer front.
2. Use a 1/4" flat brush to paint maroon checks on the upper left and lower right and pink checks on the upper right and lower left. Let dry.
3. Use a liner brush to paint tiny dots where the checks meet – sage dots on maroon and mustard checks, midnight blue dots on pink and mustard checks.
4. Paint a frame around the areas where the drawer pulls will be with sage. Outline inside of frame with midnight blue.
5. Paint a border around the drawer and dividing lines between the two check colors with sage.

Decorate Tops of Legs:

1. With a small round brush, paint rings of various sizes with lime sherbet. See Fig. 1b.
2. On a few rings, highlight with mustard. See Fig. 1c.
3. Place a few dots with midnight blue where the rings meet. See Fig. 1d.

Decorate the Top:

1. Dilute brown paint with a little water. Brush on streaks over the mustard base paint. See Fig. 2b. Let dry.
2. Sponge on a little charcoal, dragging the sponge in a few places. See Figs. 2c and 2d.
3. Measure and mask off 3/4"-wide stripes 2" from edges of top. Paint with pink. Remove tape. Let dry. *Tip:* Mask off and paint the stripes on the left and right, let dry completely, then mask off and paint stripes on front and back.

Antique:

Mix an antiquing stain of two parts neutral glazing medium and one part brown paint. Brush over entire surface of table with a sponge brush. Let dry.

Finish:

1. Seal the surface with several coats of waterbase varnish. Let dry between coats.
2. Install drawer pulls. ❑

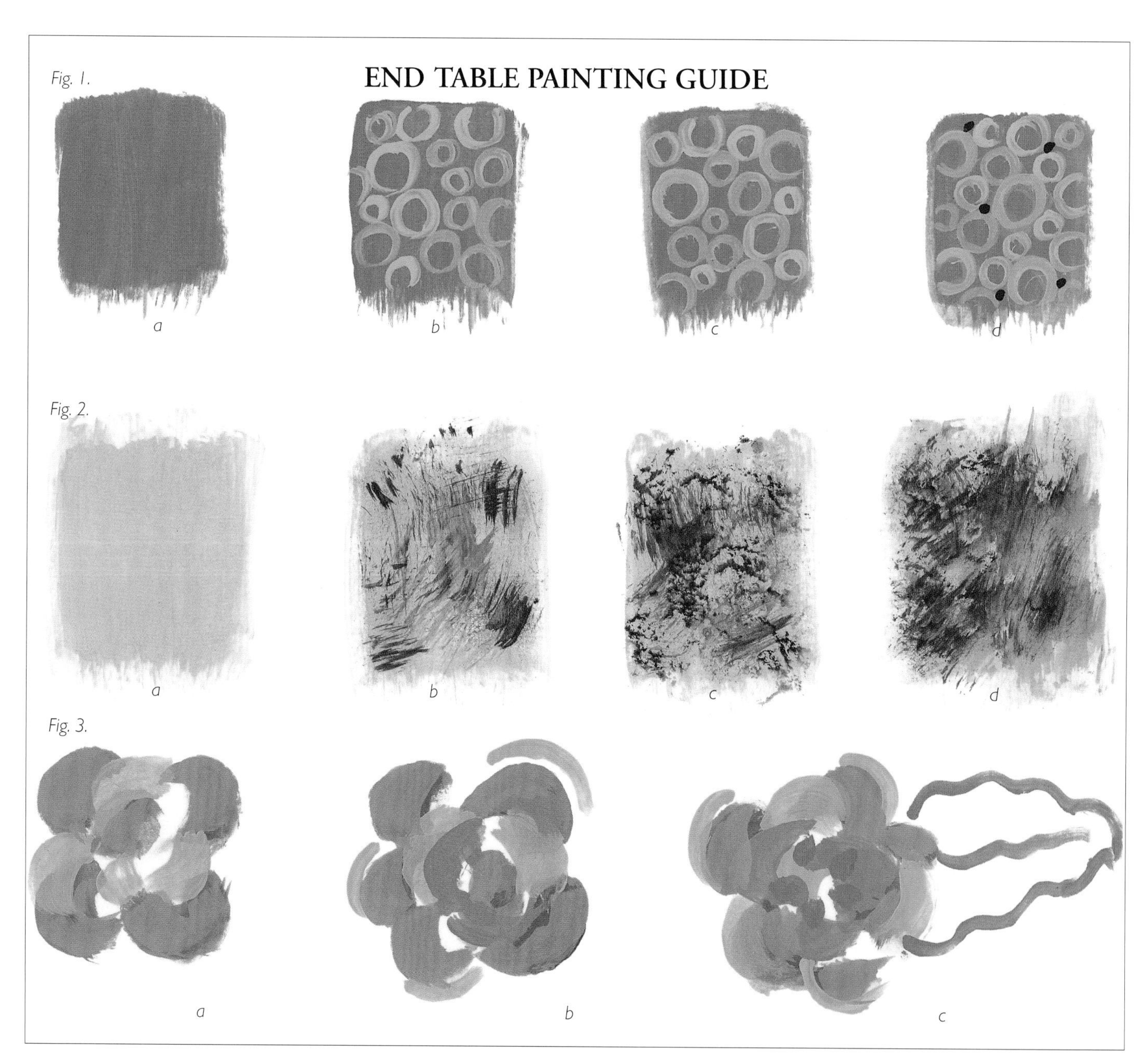

OLD WORLD TILES

dining table

Lustrous metallic paints are applied to taped-off diamonds over the entire top of a dining room table to give the look of sumptuous tiles. Stamped circles, created with a pencil eraser, accent the corners of the "tiles."

Created by Kathi Malarchuk Bailey

Techniques Used: Decorative painting, stamping

SUPPLIES

Surface:
Oval wooden dining table

Paint:
Black latex, flat or satin finish
Acrylic craft paints – Metallic gold, metallic silver, metallic copper, metallic blue

Other Supplies:
Masking tape, 1/4" wide (sometimes sold as "grout tape")
Ruler
Pencil with new flat, eraser
Foam brushes
Foam plates (for palette)
Sandpaper
Waterbase varnish, gloss sheen

INSTRUCTIONS

Prepare:
Prepare table for painting, following instructions in the "Preparation" section.

Base Paint:
Paint tabletop and legs with two (or more) coats of black latex paint. Let dry and sand between coats.

Paint Design:
1. Measure and mark a 2" border around edge of tabletop. Mask off with 1/4" tape. (The narrow tape works better on curves than 3/4" or 1" tape).
2. Mask off a 1/4" border inside the 2" border.
3. Measure width and length of table inside border and determine center point. Starting at center point, measure and mark 4" diamonds across entire tabletop. Mask off lines with 1/4" tape.
4. Paint diamonds with metallic paints, alternating colors. Two coats may be required for solid coverage. Let dry.

Finish:
1. Paint 1/4" border with metallic silver.
2. Paint trim edge of table (if your table has this feature) with metallic gold. Let dry and remove tape.
3. Dip end of pencil eraser in metallic gold paint. Dot at corners of each diamond. Let dry 24-48 hrs.
4. Seal with several coats of waterbase varnish. Let dry between coats. ❑

FLOWER BOUQUET

octagonal pedestal table

A bright bouquet of flowers spreads color over the top of this octagonal table. The pedestal base includes a variety of simple handpainted designs and an interesting interplay of colors. A Painting Guide is included for the designs on the pedestal. This special table adorns a breakfast room – what a way to wake up!

Created by Lindsey Mahaffey

Techniques Used: Decorative painting

SUPPLIES

Surface:
Octagonal wooden pedestal table, 18" on each edge, 47" across, 29" high

Acrylic Craft Paint:
Black
Blue
Brown
Cream
Green
Lavender
Orange
Purple
Red
Teal
White
Yellow

Other Supplies:
An assortment of artist's brushes, including rounds, flats (1", 1/2"), and liners
Foam or bristle brushes for base painting
Straight edge (such as a yardstick)
Pencil
Masking tape
Waterbase varnish, gloss sheen

INSTRUCTIONS

Prepare:
Prepare table for painting and prime, following instructions in "Preparation" section.

Paint Top:
1. Use a straight edge and pencil to draw lines to connect points of the octagon so the lines create triangles that meet in the center of the tabletop.
2. Paint every other triangle with black. Let dry.
3. Paint remaining triangles with cream. Let dry.
4. Use a small round brush to paint small black triangles along the outer edges of the cream triangles and small cream triangles along the outer edges of the black triangles. Let dry.
5. Paint the outer edge of the tabletop with red, using a 1/2" flat brush.
6. Paint table apron with green. Let dry. Use a flat brush to paint evenly spaced vertical black stripes.
7. Trace and transfer pattern for flower bouquet.

Decorate Top:
Instructions for painting the flowers begin with the big purple pansy at top right, and work clockwise around the bouquet from there.
1. Purple pansy – Paint with purple, mixing in blue to darken the shaded areas and adding white to lighten the outer edges. Paint the center with black.
2. Blue daisy – Paint petals with blue. While paint is still wet, lighten the interiors of the petals by mixing in some white, leaving a darker blue outline. Shade around center with black. Paint center with yellow.
3. Red lily – Use red mixed with streaks of yellow to create the pointed petals. Shade near the center and where the petals overlap with black.
4. Poppy – Paint petals with red. Outline loosely with black. Add loose streaks of orange.
5. Yellow lily – Paint petals with yellow. Use brown to shade and white to highlight. Add a faint white line down the center of each petals to add dimension. Paint center with black.
6. Four-petal flower – Paint with purple. Shade with black. Lighten around the edges with white.
7. Primrose cluster – Paint petals with rough circles of blue. Paint centers with yellow. Dot each center with black. Add black squiggly lines to petals.
8. Dark pink tulip – Paint basic shape with red. Outline inner edges of petals with black. Blend in streaks of white to lighten each petal.

Continued on page 82

continued from page 80

9. Blue lily – Paint the six petals with blue, blending a tiny bit of black and white into each petal. (This will result in a mixture of blue, light blue, and blue gray.) Re-define the outer edges with blue. Paint center with black. Dot center with white.
10. Tiger lily – Paint petals with yellow and streak with red. Use a small pointed brush to create dots with black on the lower half of each petal. In the center, paint more black dots, overlapping them with white dots.
11. Red zinnia – Paint with red. Use black to darken the ring at the center and to define each petal. Lighten petals with a bit of yellow. Paint center with yellow.
12. Buds – Paint with yellow. Streak lightly with brown and green.
13. Purple petunia – Paint petals with Purple. Define the petals with lines of blue.
14. Violet – Paint petals with a series of purple half-moon shapes. Define petal shapes with black and white lines. Add yellow to the center.
15. Magnolia blossom – Outline with black and fill in with cream, allowing the black to blend into the cream. Layer yellow, black, and white dots in the center.
16. Blue carnation – Outline each petal with blue. Paint the base of each petal with black, the middle with blue, and the outer edge with white, then blend.
17. Pink hibiscus – Paint petals with red and blend in white to turn petals pink, letting red streaks show through. Add yellow dots in the center.
18. Pink tulip – Paint petals with white and blend in pink for definition.
19. Yellow tulip – Paint petals with yellow and blend in red for definition.
20. Blue pom poms – Paint with teal. While paint is still wet, add small white dots for texture.
21. Marigold – Outline each petal with red mixed with a little black. Paint each petal with yellow, blending with the dark red of the outline. Dot center with dark red (red + black).
22. Leaves & stems – Paint with green. Shade with brown.

Paint Pedestal:

The pedestal is painted with a different design on each section of the turned pedestal. Adapt the designs to fit your table. The numbers of the instructions are keyed to the figure numbers on the Painting Guide.

1. Base paint with black. Add wavy vertical lines of cream.
2. Base paint with red. Add scallops with yellow. Accent with black, alternating strokes and dots as shown.
3. Base paint with purple. Add wavy diamond shapes with lavender. Paint s-strokes with blue. Add additional strokes of blue to accent.
4. Base paint with green. Mix black and green to make a dark green. Paint narrow vertical stripes.
5. Base paint with black. Paint a peaked border with cream.
6. Base paint with yellow. Paint a vine-and-leaf border with green. Accent with dots of teal. Outline dots with green.
7. Base paint with yellow. Paint wide black vertical stripes. Outline stripes with thin red lines.
8. Paint inner part of feet with yellow. Use a 1/2" flat brush to paint checks with black. Outline with red. Paint edges with black. Let dry completely.

Finish:

Apply several coats of gloss waterbase varnish to protect the painting. Let dry between coats. ❑

PEDESTAL PAINTING GUIDE

Fig. 1

Fig. 6

Fig. 2

Fig. 7

Fig. 3

Fig. 8

Fig. 4

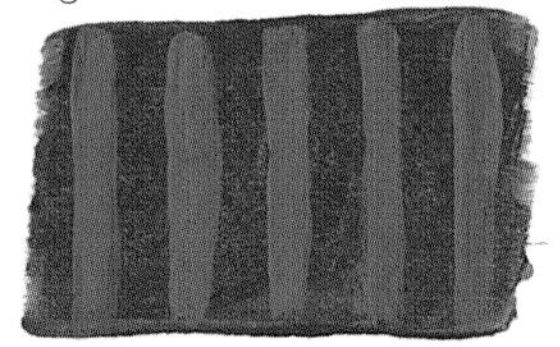

Fig. 5

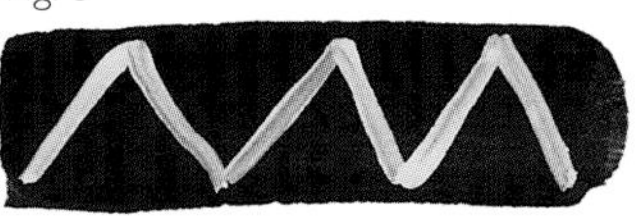

Pattern for Flower Bouquet Table

Enlarge @ 145% for Actual Size

Chests of Drawers

No one ever has enough space for stashing things. A chest of drawers, painted brightly, is a wonderful way to hide all that "stuff" we think we need to have. Whether in the bedroom, bathroom, or kitchen – make it a piece that garners compliments. There are so many ways to add interest to chests of drawers. The four projects in this section showcase painting, stenciling, staining, and sponging with a wealth of ideas and styles – playful, rustic, and refined.

Pictured at right: *Daisies & Ladybugs Miniature Chest. Instructions begin on page 90.*

DAISIES & LADYBUGS

miniature chest

Painted wooden cutouts accent and enliven this small chest of drawers, originally an unfinished furniture piece.

Created by Jeff McWilliams

Techniques Used: Sponging, decorative painting

SUPPLIES

Surface:
Wooden three-drawer jewelry chest

Acrylic Craft Paint:
Black
White
Sunny yellow
Green
Lipstick red
Christmas red

Other Supplies:
32 wooden football shapes (for petals) or cut your own petal shapes from 1/4" birch wood using pattern provided
7 wooden apples (for flower centers)
7 split eggs (for ladybugs)
Wood glue
Matte spray sealer
Foam brushes
2" bristle brush
Artist's paint brushes – flats, rounds, and liners of various sizes
Sandpaper
Sea sponge
Masking tape, 1" wide

INSTRUCTIONS

Prepare:
Remove the drawers and drawer pulls. Prepare surface, following the instructions in the "Preparation" section.

Paint the Chest:
1. Paint the chest with two coats white paint. Let dry and sand between coats.
2. Dry brush the front, back, sides and drawer fronts of the chest with green paint, using very little paint on a 2" bristle brush.
3. Paint the drawer pulls and feet green.
4. Paint the top and base of the chest with sunny yellow. Let dry.
5. Mask off top and base of chest. Dampen sea sponge and squeeze out excess water. Lightly sponge top and base with Christmas red, allowing some of the sunny yellow to show through.

Paint the Trim Pieces:
1. Paint the wooden football shapes (the petals) with white. Let dry. Sand and recoat.
2. Paint the wooden apples (the flower centers) with sunny yellow. Let dry. Sand and recoat.
3. Paint the split eggs (the ladybugs) with lipstick red. Let dry. Sand and recoat.
4. Paint the narrow end of the split eggs (the ladybugs' heads) with black. Paint a line down the back and add dots with black, using photo as a guide. Let dry.

Finish:
1. Using the photo as a guide, glue the flower centers and petals in place.
2. Again using the photo as a guide, glue the ladybugs in place. Allow to dry.
3. Spray with matte sealer. Let dry. ❑

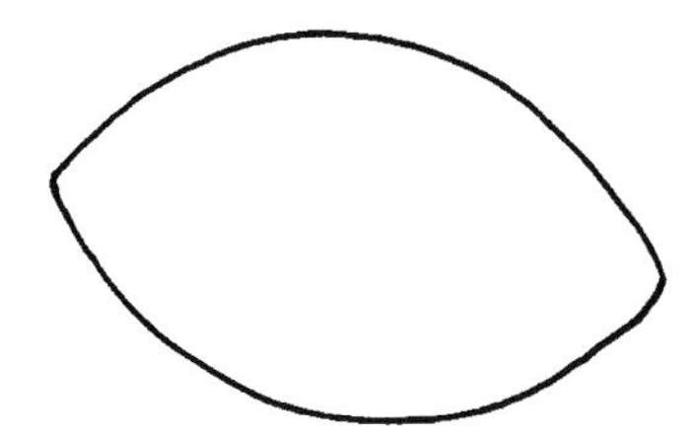

Actual Pattern for Flower Petal

Cut 32 from 1/4" birch wood

Medallions & Vines

double chest of drawers

A plain side-by-side chest is given an elegant turn with classic vine-and-leaf motifs. The stenciled and painted designs and drawer borders are created with acrylic craft paints. Brass drawer pulls complete the look.

Created by Kathi Malarchuk Bailey

Techniques Used: Stenciling, decorative painting

Instructions follow on page 94.

Medallions & Vines

SUPPLIES

Surface:
Wooden dresser

Paint:
Latex paint, flat finish – soft yellow
Acrylic craft paints, 2 oz. bottles – medium yellow green, deep yellow, rust, black

Other Supplies:
Stencil blank material
Stencil brush
Artist's paint brushes – #3 round, liner
Foam brushes
Craft knife
Fine tip permanent marker
Masking tape
Foam plates (for palette)
Sandpaper
Matte sealer spray

INSTRUCTIONS

Prepare:
Remove drawer pulls. Clean and prepare chest for painting as needed, following instructions in the "Preparation" section.

Paint:
1. Base paint entire chest with two coats soft yellow latex paint. Let dry and sand between coats.
2. Mask off a border 3/4" wide around each drawer.
3. Mask off borders 3/4" wide around the top and sides of chest approximately 1/2" from edges. Line up the upper and lower borders on the sides with the borders on drawers.
4. Paint borders with two coats deep yellow acrylic paint. Remove tape and let dry.

Stencil Motifs:
Before tracing and cutting stencils, be sure the pattern fits your drawers. If too large or too small, enlarge or reduce patterns on photocopier.
1. Trace stencil patterns provided on stencil blank material with a fine tip permanent marker.
2. Using a craft knife, cut out stencils.
3. Stencil medallion with deep yellow at center of each large drawer, middle small drawer, center of top, and upper center of each side.
4. Stencil leaf branch in deep yellow on each side of medallion on large drawers, above medallion on sides, and individually on small drawers.
5. Mask off part of stencil to fit on each side of medallion on small drawer and stencil.
6. Stencil leaf branch in oval around medallion on top of dresser. Add one leaf branch on each side of oval on top.

Embellish with Paint:
1. Dilute medium yellow green with water, using three parts paint to one part water. Use a round brush to lightly wash leaves on leaf branches and leaf sections of medallion.
2. Dilute rust acrylic with water, using three parts paint to one part water. Use a round brush to lightly wash over flowers on medallion.
3. Dilute black paint with an equal amount of water. Using a liner brush, outline all leaf branches and medallions.

Stencil Borders:
Mix equal amounts of medium yellow green and deep yellow. Stencil leaf border just inside the deep yellow borders on all drawers, on both sides, and on top. Let dry.

Finish:
1. Seal with matte sealer. Let dry.
2. Install drawer pulls. ❑

Actual Size Patterns

Leaf Border

Medallion

Leaf Branch

FAUX PARQUET

stained wooden chest

This chest uses three colors of wood stain to create the look of parquet. The design combines stripes and triangles – stripes on the door and sides and triangles on the drawer fronts, drawer pulls, and top. Smaller triangles form the border around the base and the upper panel.

Created by Susan Goans Driggers

Techniques Used: Staining

SUPPLIES

Surface:
Wooden chest

Stain:
3 colors wood stain, such as natural, oak, and walnut

Other Supplies:
Pencil & ruler
Fine tip permanent marker with dark brown or black ink
Flat brushes and/or sponge brushes
Soft cloth rags
Masking tape
Matte sealer spray
Waterbase varnish

INSTRUCTIONS

Prepare:
Remove door and drawer pulls. Prepare chest for staining, following instructions in the "Preparation" section.

Stain the Background:
Stain the entire chest with the stain color you've chosen to be your background (the lightest of the three colors), following manufacturer's instructions. Let dry.

Draw & Ink the Design:
1. Using the photo as a guide, adapt the design to work with your chest.
2. Draw the design on the surface, using a pencil and ruler.
3. Ink the design lines, using a fine tip marker. Let dry.

Stain the Design:
1. Mask off around the elements of the design that you plan to stain one of the other colors.
2. Stain those design elements, using a brush to apply the stain. Keep the brush fairly dry as you work – if you use too much stain you risk the stain seeping or smearing. Carefully wipe away any excess stain. Let dry. Remove tape. *Tip:* Practice staining a piece of similar wood before working on your chest.
3. Mask off around the elements of the design that you plan to stain the third color.
4. Stain those elements. Let dry. Remove tape.
5. Use the same techniques to add borders or decorative accents. Let dry completely.

Finish:
1. Spray the chest lightly with matte sealer. Let dry.
2. Apply several coats of waterbase varnish. Let dry between coats. ❑

Trout Fantasy

chest of drawers

This small chest could be used as an end table or a nightstand. My husband ties his own flies, so he has chosen it to reside in a section of our den that has become his fly tying studio. It will hold all those feathers, hides, glues, and other smelly stuff that he uses to create his wonderful works of art. The stained base and fish and lure motifs give a rustic look. The brushed nickel pulls recall the finish of fishing gear.

Created by Kirsten Jones

Techniques Used: Stenciling, staining, sponging

Supplies

Surface:
Wooden three-drawer chest

Acrylic Craft Paint:
Sterling blue
Teal green
Summer sky
Gray green
Italian sage

Other Supplies:
Gel wood stain – aged oak
Old rags or staining sponge
Pre-cut stencil with large fish and lures
Sea sponge
Stencil tape
Fine tip black permanent marker
Gloss sealer
3 brushed nickel drawer pulls

Instructions

Prepare:
Remove drawers and drawer pulls, if any. Prepare chest for staining, following instructions in "Preparation" section.

Stain & Basecoat:
1. Stain entire piece (but not the drawers) with aged oak stain, following manufacturer's instructions. Let dry.
2. Base paint fronts of drawers with summer sky. Let dry.

Sponge:
1. Dampen sea sponge with water and squeeze out excess. Load sponge with sterling blue and teal green. Randomly sponge drawer fronts.
2. Rinse sponge and squeeze to remove excess water. Load sponge with Italian sage and gray green. Sponge drawer fronts to soften previous applied colors. Let dry.

Stencil:
1. Position fish stencil on drawer front and tape in place. Sponge over stencil with sterling blue and teal green at top of fish and summer sky at bottom of fish, blending the colors. Repeat on remaining drawer fronts, using photo as a guide for placement.
2. Stencil a lure with sterling blue. Let dry.

Finish:
1. Using a black fine tip marker, outline stencil designs and add details to fish.
2. Apply several coats of sealer. Let dry.
3. Install drawer pulls. ❏

Cabinets

Cabinets are the perfect storage solution for almost any room. Large or small, there is usually plenty of area to decorate. The four examples in this section range from playful to sophisticated, creating versatile storage options.

Pictured at right: *Golden Vines Armoire. Instructions begin on page 102.*

GOLDEN VINES

armoire

The gold-leafed designs on this elegant armoire were created with stencils, using leaf adhesive – rather than paint – to stencil the motifs. Sheets of gold leafing were applied over the adhesive. This armoire is the perfect solution for hiding the television.

Created by Kathi Malarchuk Bailey

Techniques Used: Stenciling, gold leafing

SUPPLIES

Surface:
Wooden cupboard

Paint:
Latex paint, flat finish – black
Acrylic craft paint – metallic antique gold

Brushes:
Foam brushes
Stencil brush
Soft brush for gold leafing

Other Tools & Supplies:
Stencil blank material
Gold leaf
Metal leaf adhesive
Clear glass knob
Masking tape
Black permanent marker
Craft knife
Ruler & pencil
Wax paper
Foam plates (for palette)
Spray matte sealer

INSTRUCTIONS

Prepare:
Clean and prepare cupboard as needed, following instructions in the "Preparation" section.

Paint:
1. Base paint cupboard except door with two coats black latex paint. Let dry and sand between coats.
2. Base paint door with two coats antique gold. Let dry thoroughly.
3. Mask off a 1" border on sides of cupboard that is 2-1/2" inside the edges. Mask off a 1" border on front that is 1" around door.
4. Paint borders with two coats antique gold. Remove tape and let dry.
5. Mask off a border 3/8" wide on door 1" from outer edge.
6. Paint border with two coats black. Remove tape and let dry.

Prepare Stencil:
1. Trace or photocopy pattern from book and make sure the complete pattern fits your cupboard. If too large or small, enlarge or reduce pattern on copier.
2. Trace adjusted pattern on stencil blank material with black marker. Cut out stencil with a craft knife.
3. Tape complete stencil to top section of cupboard, making sure it is flat. *Note:* ***Do not*** use stencil adhesive to secure stencil to surface – the adhesive may leave a residue to which gold leafing will adhere.

Apply Gold Leafing:
1. Apply leaf adhesive with stencil brush to openings of stencil. Remove stencil and let adhesive set up 20-30 minutes or according to manufacturer's instructions.
2. Carefully lift sheets of gold leafing and place over stenciled areas. Lay a sheet of wax paper over gold leafing and lightly rub the area to be sure the leaf is well adhered. Continue applying leafing until all adhesive is covered. Dust away excess leafing with a soft brush. Clean adhesive from stencil before continuing.
3. Mask off 1" border around entire door, using photo as a guide. Apply leaf adhesive to border area. Let adhesive set up. Apply gold leafing to adhesive. Brush away excess.
4. Mask off clean stencil to allow stenciling of large leaf, small leaf, and small flower individually. Randomly stencil design elements on door and below door with leaf adhesive, using photo as a guide for placement. Let adhesive set up. Apply gold leafing to adhesive. Brush away excess.

Finish:
1. Seal with Matte Sealer. Let dry.
2. Install glass knob on door. ❑

Actual Size Patterns

THREE OLIVES, PLEASE!

martini cabinet

This cabinet was painted black and decorated with metallic paints for a dramatic art deco ambience. Use it to store your martini glasses and – of course – plenty of olives.

Created by Jeff McWilliams

Techniques Used: Decorative painting, sponging

SUPPLIES

Surface:
Wooden window cabinet

Acrylic Craft Paint:
Black
Light green
Metallic peridot
Metallic garnet red
Metallic silver
Metallic gunmetal gray

Wooden Trim Pieces:
18 split eggs (for olives)
1 egg, 1-1/2" (for door pull)
1/8" diameter wooden dowel, 6" long (for pick)
1 wooden doll head (for pick trim)

Other Supplies:
Artist's paint brushes – flats of various sizes
Foam brushes
Drill & 1/8" drill bit
Sandpaper, fine grit
Wood glue
Cellulose sponge
Gloss spray sealer

INSTRUCTIONS

Prepare:
1. Prepare cabinet according to the instructions in the "Preparation" section.
2. Using the drill and 1/8" drill bit, drill a hole at an angle through the 1-1/2" egg.
3. Sand the ends of the dowel.

Paint the Cabinet:
1. Paint interior or cabinet with light green.
2. Paint the exterior of the cabinet, including the window muntins, with black. Let dry. Sand, wipe away dust, and recoat. Let dry.
3. Mask off the windows and the top. Paint window trim and top with metallic silver. Let dry.
4. Dampen cellulose sponge and squeeze out excess water. Sponge window trim and top with metallic gunmetal gray. Remove tape. Let dry.

Paint the Trim Pieces:
1. Paint the split eggs (the olives) and the 1-1/2" egg (the door pull) with metallic peridot. Let dry. Sand and recoat.
2. Paint the pimento at each end of each olive with metallic garnet red. Let dry and recoat.
3. Paint the wooden dowel (the pick) with black. Let dry.
4. Paint the doll head (the pick trim) with metallic garnet red. Let dry.

Finish:
1. Glue the pick trim to one end of the pick. Allow to dry.
2. Insert the pick in the door pull and glue to secure. Allow to dry.
3. Glue the door pull to the knob on the cabinet. Allow to dry.
4. Glue the split olives on the front and sides of the cabinet, using photo as a guide.
5. Spray with gloss sealer. Let dry. ❑

AUTUMN LEAVES

blanket chest

This rustic blanket chest is just right for bed linens or sweaters. The bouquet of stamped oak leaves, created with a purchased stamp, echo the cozy colors of autumn.

Created by Kathi Malarchuk Bailey

Techniques Used: Crackling, stamping, staining

Instructions follow on page 108

Autumn Leaves

SUPPLIES

Surface:
Unfinished wooden chest

Paint:
Latex paint, flat finish – cream white, medium brown
Acrylic craft paints – dark brown, metallic gold, light green

Tools & Other Supplies:
Crackle medium
Neutral glazing medium
Stamp – oak leaf
Masking tape
Foam brushes
Stamp applicators
Foam plates (for palette)
Sandpaper
Paper towels
Pencil & ruler
Unfinished wood knob with screw
Drill
Spray matte sealer

INSTRUCTIONS

Preparation:
Prepare wooden chest for painting, following instructions in the "Preparation" section.

Paint & Stain:
1. Mask off legs. Base paint remainder of chest with two coats cream white latex. Let dry and sand lightly between coats. Remove tape from legs. Let dry.
2. Paint top and bottom trim, using photo as a guide, with two coats dark brown acrylic.
3. Mix a small amount of dark brown acrylic with an equal amount of neutral glazing medium. Stain legs with glaze mixture, using a foam brush to apply and wiping with paper towels to remove excess. Let dry.

Crackle:
1. Mask off trim areas and legs. Mask off an 8" x 10" rectangle on lower front of chest.
2. Apply crackle medium to top and sides of chest, following manufacturer's instructions. Let dry.
3. Apply medium brown latex paint as top coat to crackle, following "Crackling" instructions in the "Techniques" section. Remove tape and let dry completely.

Create Stamped Panel:
1. Mask off a border 3/8" wide around cream rectangle on front. Paint border with two coats metallic gold. Remove tape and let dry.
2. Mask off a second 3/8" border outside the gold border. Paint with two coats dark brown acrylic. Paint wooden knob with dark brown acrylic. Remove all tape. Let dry.
3. Stamp oak leaves with metallic gold, dark brown, and light green acrylic paints, using photo as a guide for placement. Let dry.

Finish:
1. Drill hole in front upper center, using photo as a guide, and attach painted wood knob.
2. Spray with matte sealer. ❑

PEAS & CARROTS

miniature cabinet

This crackled cabinet with brightly painted trim is a reminder to us all to eat our vegetables. Painted wooden cutouts add dimension. It would be great in a kitchen or breakfast room.

Created by Jeff McWilliams

Techniques Used: Crackling, decorative painting

SUPPLIES

Surface:
Wall cabinet

Acrylic Craft Paint:
White
Kelly green
Green
Sunny yellow
Orange
Magenta

Wooden Trim Pieces:
15 wooden pea shapes
45 wooden hole caps (peas)
11 wooden carrot shapes

Other Supplies:
Artist's paint brushes – flats in various sizes
Sandpaper, fine grit
Crackle medium
Foam brushes
Black fine tip permanent marker
Wood glue
Gloss sealer spray

INSTRUCTIONS

Prepare:
Remove door, drawers, and drawer and door pulls. Prepare cabinet, following instructions in the "Preparation" section.

Paint & Crackle the Cabinet:
1. Paint the front, sides, and back of cabinet and the inside of the door with sunny yellow. Let dry. Sand and recoat. Let dry.
2. Apply crackle medium to sides, back, and front of the cabinet. Let dry.
3. Brush over the crackle medium with white. Cracks will form. Let dry.
4. Paint the top and base of the cabinet with kelly green. Let dry. Sand and recoat.
5. Paint the drawer fronts with magenta.
6. Paint the door frame and hinges with green. Let dry.

Paint the Trim Pieces:
1. Paint the door and drawer pulls with kelly green. Paint the pea shapes with kelly green.
2. Paint the hole caps (peas) with green.
3. Paint the carrots with orange. Let dry. Paint the carrot stems and leaves with kelly green. Let dry.

Finish:
1. Trace and transfer the lettering to the door, using photo as a guide for placement. Go over the lettering with a black marker.
2. Glue three peas to each pea shape.
3. Glue peas to sides and front of cabinet, using photo as a guide for placement. Allow to dry.
4. Glue carrots on the drawers, using photo as a guide for placement. Allow to dry.
5. Install door and drawer pulls.
6. Spray with gloss sealer. Let dry. ❑

Eat your Peas and Carrots
Eat Your Peas
Eat Your Peas and Carrots
Eat your Peas and Carrots

Especially for Kids

This section includes painted furniture projects especially for kids, painted on kid-size furniture. These pieces are sure to become heirlooms, treasured for years by generations to come.

If you don't feel comfortable painting an armoire for your living room, then choosing a small piece of furniture to paint for a favorite child is the perfect way to experience yourself. No matter how your first efforts look, the child will think it is beautiful.

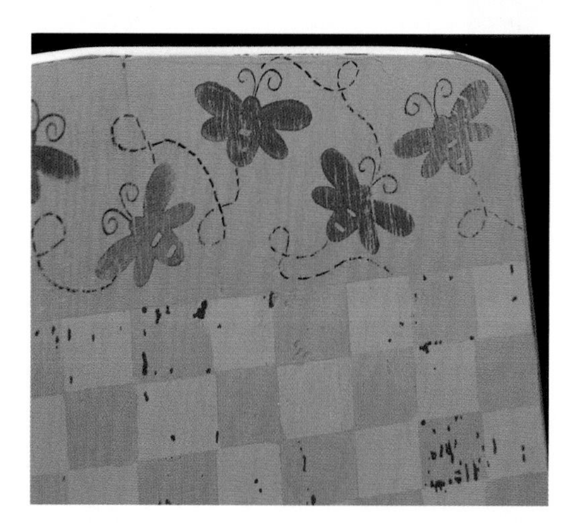

Pictured at right: *Fantasy Patchwork Table & Chair Set. Instructions begin on page 114.*

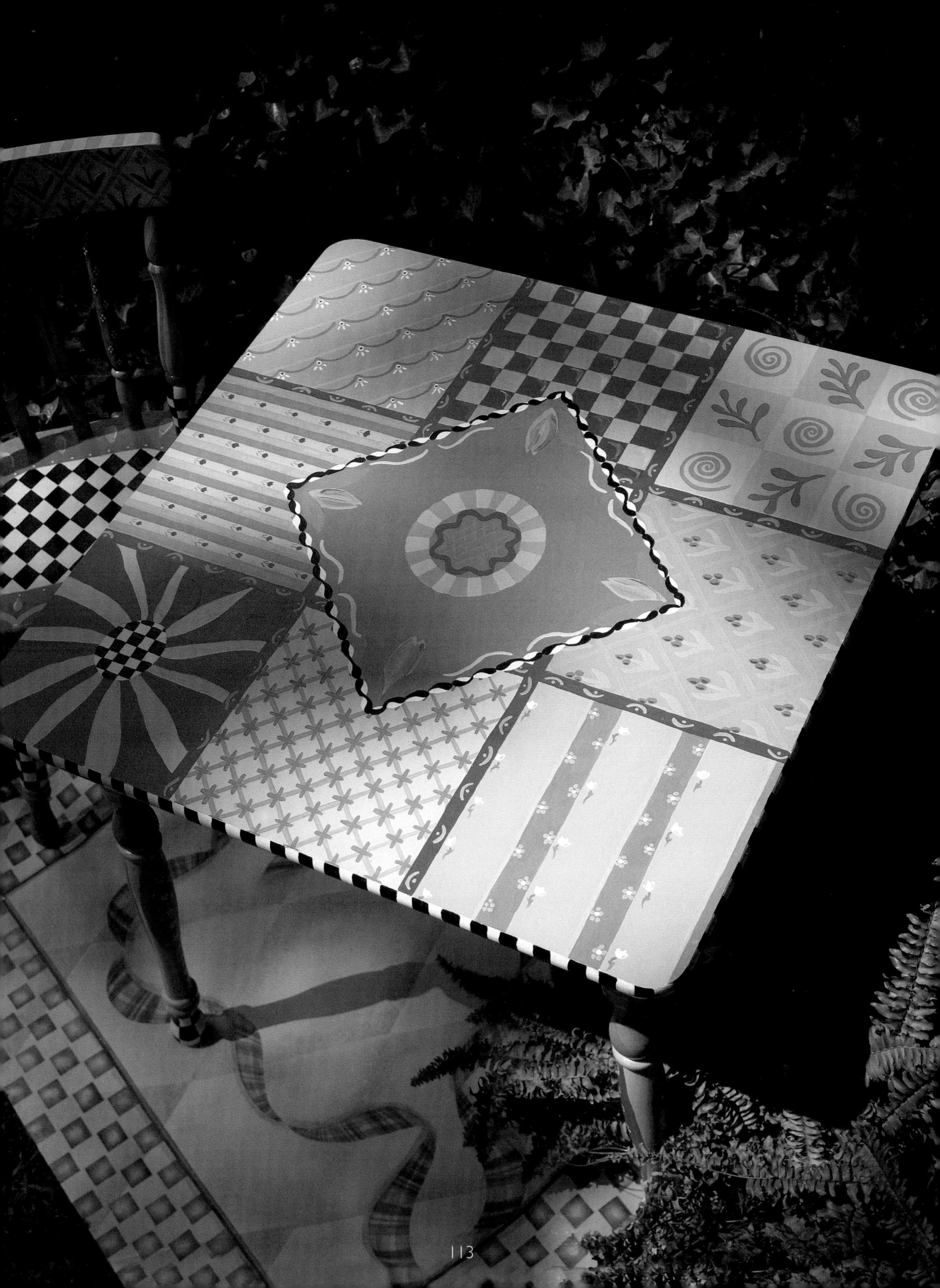

Fantasy Patchwork

child's table & chair set

An array of simple designs in clear colors are combined like patchwork to delight the eye and enliven a child's room. Choose designs from the patterns provided or use them as inspirations for a personal patchwork all your own.

Created by Kelley Noorbakhsh

Technique Used: Decorative painting

Supplies

Surface:
Children's table and chairs

Acrylic Craft Paint:
Black
Bright magenta
Buttercup
Hot pink
Lavender
Leaf green
Light pink
Lilac dust
Mauve
Pale peach
Sky blue
Valentine pink
Victorian green
White

Other Supplies:
Transfer paper & stylus
Masking tape
Ruler & pencil
Artist's paint brushes – flats, rounds, and liners of various sizes
Waterbase varnish

Instructions follow on page 116

FROGS

INSTRUCTIONS

Prepare:

1. Clean and prepare table and chairs for painting as needed, following instructions in the "Preparation" section.
2. Measure and mark nine squares of equal size on the tabletop.
3. Measure and mark the center point of the table. From that center point, measure and mark the center diamond shape. (This one is an 11" square.) Mask off inside the diamond shape.
4. Measure and mark the insets on the chair seats.
5. Choose designs from the patterns provided and the project photos for the eight patchwork squares on the periphery of the table and the chair insets or draw your own designs on paper.

Paint the Backgrounds on the Tabletop & Chair Seats:

1. Paint the backgrounds of the squares, using the paint colors listed with the patterns or with colors of your choosing. Let dry.
2. Transfer your chosen designs to the squares. If you want to create checkerboards, you can paint them freehand or mask them off with tape.

Paint the Designs:

1. Paint the designs, using the paint colors listed with the pattern or with colors of your choosing. Remove tape. Let dry overnight.
2. Mask off the center diamond on the table. Paint with valentine pink or the color of your choice. Let dry.
3. Transfer the design.
4. Paint the design, using the paint colors listed with the patterns or with colors of your choosing. Remove tape. Let dry overnight.
5. Mask off the borders that separate the squares on the tabletop. Paint with hot pink or the color of your choice. Remove tape. Let dry.
6. Embellish the border, using the Dot & Scallop Border pattern.

Paint the Trim:

1. Select colors and designs for the table and chair legs, chair backs and spindles, table apron, and edges, using the photos as guides for color placement and design ideas. Paint, masking off as needed. Let dry.
2. Embellish with designs of your choice from the patterns supplied or your own inspirations. Let dry.

Finish:

Apply several coats of waterbase varnish to protect. Let dry between coats. ❑

Actual Size Pattern for Table & Chairs

Leaf & Spiral Square
Background – Buttercup, Victorian green
Spirals – Sky blue
Leaves – Leaf green

Patterns for Table & Chairs

Flowers & Diamond Square
Background – Mauve
Diamond lines – Pale peach
Leaves – Buttercup
Petals – Valentine pink
Petal accents – Hot pink

FROGS

Actual Size Patterns for Table & Chairs

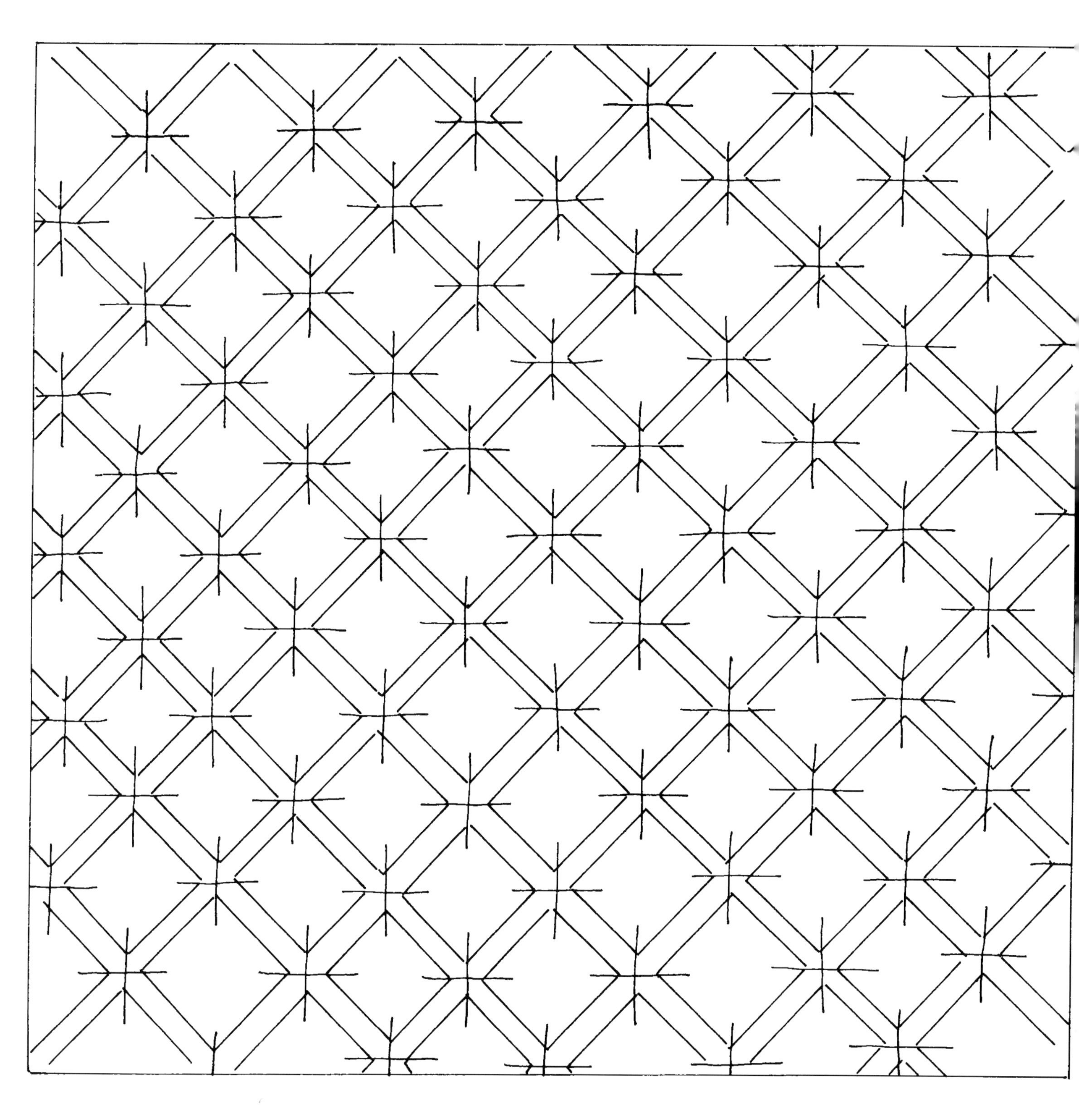

Lattice & Cross Square
Background – Victorian green
Lattice – Sky blue
Crosses – Leaf green

Flower Swag Border
Swag – Victorian green
Swag dots – White
Leaves – Leaf green
Flowers – Pale peach with white accents

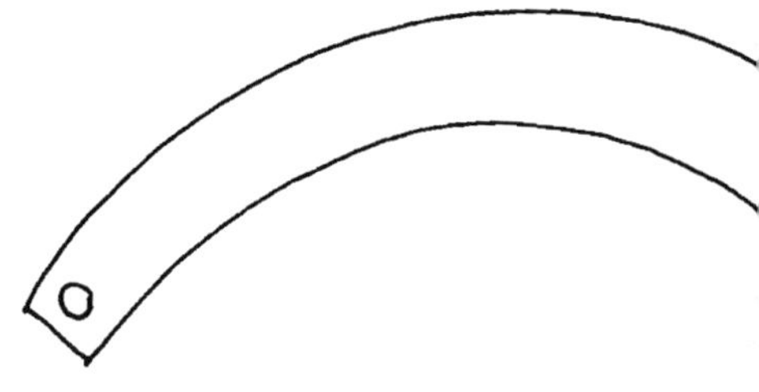

Center Circle
Background – Valentine pink
Outer ring – Buttercup, sky blue
Outer wave – Hot pink
Inner wave – Lilac dust
Center lines – Leaf green

Border Designs

Dot & Scallop Border
Background – Hot pink
Dots & scallops – Sky blue

Tiny Flowers Border
Centers – White or bright magenta
Petals – Sky blue or white

Checks & Bees

baby's high chair

The distressed finish of this high chair has the look of an instant antique. It's a great way to dress up a tired hand-me-down and give it a soft new look.

Created by Kathi Malarchuk Bailey

Techniques Used: Distressing, stamping, decorative painting

Supplies

Surface:
Wooden high chair

Paint:
Latex paint, flat finish – light yellow, soft green
Acrylic craft paints, 2 oz. bottles – bright green, black

Tools & Other Supplies:
Stamp with bee motif
Masking tape, 1" wide
Sandpaper
Handheld electric sander
Foam paint brushes
Artist's liner brush
Foam plates (for palette)
Sponge applicator for stamp
Spray matte sealer

Instructions

Prepare:
Clean and prepare chair as needed, following instructions in the "Preparation" section.

Paint:
1. Base paint chair with two coats light yellow latex paint. Let dry.
2. Mask off arms and leg stretchers. Mask off chair back 5" down from top on front and back.
3. Paint arms, leg stretchers, and top of back with two coats soft green latex paint. Let dry and remove tape.
4. To create the checkerboard and chair back and seat, mask off horizontal stripes 1" apart. Then mask off vertical stripes 1" apart. This will create the first, third, fifth, etc. rows of checks. Paint checks with soft green latex. Remove tape and let dry thoroughly.
5. To create the second, fourth, sixth, etc. rows, mask off existing rows horizontally and vertically. Paint checks with soft green latex. Remove tape and let dry thoroughly.

Stamp & Trim:
1. Apply bright green acrylic paint to bee stamp. Stamp on area at top of back of chair.
2. Dilute a small amount of black acrylic paint with an equal amount of water. Use a liner brush to paint flight lines, using photo as a guide. Let dry one hour.

Distress:
Sand edges, front, legs, and seat to distress and simulate wear and tear. Wipe away dust.

Finish:
Spray with matte sealer. Let dry. ❑

B IS FOR BUMBLEBEE

child's desk chair

A variety of paint techniques and bright cheery colors make this a special chair for a special child. It might also be the inspiration for an alphabet series!

Created by Holly Buttimer

Techniques Used: Sponging, decorative painting

SUPPLIES

Surface:
Wooden children's chair

Acrylic Craft Paint:
Black
Blue
Lavender
Lemonade
Lime
Metallic gold
Metallic antique gold
Ochre
White
Yellow

Other Supplies:
Cellulose sponge
Sponge brushes
Comb
Neutral glazing medium
3 wooden balls
Finishing nails
Wood glue
Artist's paint brushes – flats, rounds, and liners of various sizes
Waterbase varnish

INSTRUCTIONS

Prepare:
Clean and prepare chair for painting as needed, following instructions in the "Preparation" section.

Base Paint:
1. Transfer the outlines for the seat design to the chair seat.
2. Base paint the seat area inside the wavy line, the leg stretchers, the edge of the seat, and the front sides of the back slats with blue.
3. Base paint the outer area of the seat, the legs, the apron, the back uprights, and the remaining areas of the back slats with yellow. Let dry.
4. Base paint two wooden balls with blue. Base paint the remaining ball with yellow.

Comb:
1. Mix two parts lavender paint and one part neutral glazing medium.
2. Working one section at a time, brush glaze mixture over legs and back uprights. While glaze is still wet, comb through glaze to create squiggles, removing some of the glaze. Clean comb by wiping periodically with a rag. Continue until legs and uprights are complete. Let dry.

Continued on page 126

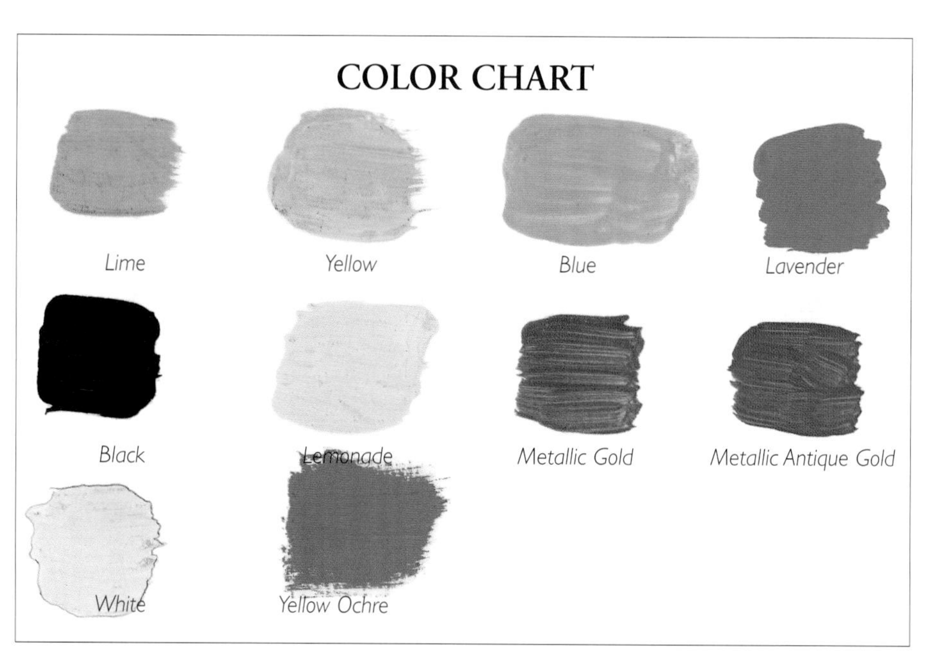

B is for Bumble Bee
FROGS
BY BEATRIX POTTER
F. WARNE & CO

continued from page 124

3. Again working one section at a time, brush glaze mixture over stretchers and seat edge. While glaze is still wet, comb through glaze to create stripes, removing some of the glaze. Clean comb by wiping periodically with a rag. Continue until stretchers and seat edge are complete. Let dry.
4. Mix two parts blue paint with one part neutral glazing medium.
5. Working one section at a time, brush glaze mixture over chair apron. While glaze is still wet, comb through glaze to create squiggles, removing some of the glaze. Clean comb periodically with a rag. Continue until apron is complete. Let dry overnight.

Streak & Sponge:

1. Using a foam brush, streak the back slats randomly with yellow. Let dry.
2. Dampen a sponge and squeeze to remove excess water. Sponge back slats randomly with lavender.

Paint the Seat Design:

1. Transfer pattern.
2. Paint the bee's body with black and yellow, using photo as a guide for color placement.
3. Shade with ochre and metallic antique gold.
4. Highlight with metallic gold and lemonade.
5. Paint wings with white.
6. Streak wings with blue and metallic gold.
7. Paint eyes with metallic antique gold. Highlight with white.
8. Add details with black.
9. Paint capital Bs with yellow.
10. Paint the dots around the seat with blue.
11. Paint lettering and outline dots with black.
12. Add a lavender dot at the center of each blue dot. Paint the squiggly border with lavender.

Paint the Back Design:

1. Transfer the design to the back slats.
2. Paint bees' bodies with black and yellow. Add dimension with metallic antique gold.
3. Paint wings with white. Let dry.
4. Add details and paint flight lines with black.

Finish:

1. Decorate wooden balls with lavender, lime, and black as shown in photo. Let dry.
2. Attach balls to seat back with finishing nails and wood glue. Let dry.
3. Apply several coats waterbase varnish. Let dry between coats. ❑

Pattern for B Is for Bumblebee

Chair Seat – Enlarge @ 250% for actual size

Flight Line Patterns – Enlarge @155% for actual size.

METRIC CONVERSION CHART

Inches to Millimeters and Centimeters

Inches	MM	CM
1/8	3	.3
1/4	6	.6
3/8	10	1.0
1/2	13	1.3
5/8	16	1.6
3/4	19	1.9
7/8	22	2.2
1	25	2.5
1-1/4	32	3.2
1-1/2	38	3.8
1-3/4	44	4.4
2	51	5.1
3	76	7.6
4	102	10.2
5	127	12.7
6	152	15.2
7	178	17.8
8	203	20.3
9	229	22.9
10	254	25.4
11	279	27.9
12	305	30.5

Yards to Meters

Yards	Meters
1/8	.11
1/4	.23
3/8	.34
1/2	.46
5/8	.57
3/4	.69
7/8	.80
1	.91
2	1.83
3	2.74
4	3.66
5	4.57
6	5.49
7	6.40
8	7.32
9	8.23
10	9.14

Index